Companions
on the Bethlehem Road

15 The Chambers, Vineyard
Abingdon OX14 3FE
brf.org.uk

Bible Reading Fellowship is a charity (233280)
and company limited by guarantee (301324),
registered in England and Wales

ISBN 978 1 80039 088 1
First published 2012
This edition published 2022
10 9 8 7 6 5 4 3 2 1 0
All rights reserved

A catalogue record for this book is available from the British Library

Printed and bound by CPI Group (UK) Ltd, Croydon CR0 4YY

Companions
on the
Bethlehem Road

RACHEL BOULDING

This book is dedicated to my mother,
Joyce Boulding,
for everything, really.

With thanks
to those who have generously donated
towards the costs of this project

Contents

❧ WEEK 5: Back to the new life

❧ ❧

Acknowledgements

I would like to thank my family, friends and colleagues for helping me with this book: my husband Martin and my son Thomas for their contributions and patience when I was preoccupied; Alison Shell and Arnold Hunt for their suggestions about poetry, and particularly Alison for writing *Shakespeare and Religion* (Arden/Methuen Drama, 2010); and the staff of the *Church Times* editorial department for many stimulating conversations about faith and theology, especially Glyn Paflin and Sue Chisholm. Thanks are due, too, to Naomi Starkey of BRF, who first suggested this book, and to her colleague Lisa Cherrett, who has helped greatly with the work.

Introduction

What poets can show us

And here in dust and dirt, O here
The lilies of His love appear!
From 'The Revival' by Henry Vaughan (1621–95)

'It's been a journey.' I'm told that this has become the standard reflection of TV talent – and reality-show contestants to describe the change in their life – going from being one among thousands of hopeful performers to becoming a star (for a few minutes, at least). The idea of life as a journey is around everywhere you go. It's an ancient concept, going back many thousands of years and found in many cultures, but it seems to speak to us now more loudly than ever. Perhaps this is because we feel less settled and rooted in any particular place, as more of us have to travel to study and find work; and, of course, computers and the internet have made physical space less important in some ways. I'd like to think that the popularity of the idea could suggest that we are more open to fresh thinking, that we are keen to learn about new places and through encounters with new people.

Also, we have 'no continuing city, but we seek one to come' (Hebrews 13:14, KJV).

Inevitably, this could have its downside, if we are a feather for every wind that blows – 'tossed to and fro, and carried about with every wind of doctrine, by the sleight of men, and cunning craftiness' (Ephesians 4:14, KJV) – and susceptible to all sorts of dangerous influences. In this book, though, I want to think about the positive possibilities of hearing from voices that may be old, dead and from the past, but may be new to us and helpful in our journey. They could be famous names but perhaps known only as vague historical figures. So we've heard of Shakespeare and Tennyson but we're not as familiar with their work as we feel we ought to be – and perhaps we haven't thought that they could be helpful in our faith. We might be able to quote ''Tis better to have loved and lost / Than never to have loved at all', but perhaps we don't know where these lines first appeared, and we've never sought them out for spiritual guidance. (I've heard these lines quoted to comfort people after breaking up with a girlfriend or boyfriend, which is a long way from their original context.)

I want to suggest that poetry can be enormously helpful in our journey of faith. The poets' finely honed words have much to say to us, right now. They might come from very different ages and backgrounds, but they faced the same questions that we do – about God, human love and the problem of suffering, for example. They have often thought about these questions more deeply than most of us do, and their works endure because the fruit of their reflection still speaks vividly to so many of us.

So I'm keen to draw on the craft and expertise of a range of poets, in ways that can inform our faith. This isn't in any way a study of the poets' lives or an examination of their work, but it is a search to see what they can tell us. In many ways, I'm being unfair to them in quarrying their writing for my own purposes, for none of them wrote specifically in order to deepen the faith of 21st-century Christians. They were writing about particular subjects in the way that seemed best to them at the time. But I have found great riches in their work and would like to share these treasures. The poets almost certainly didn't intend their work to be approached in this way, but they might be glad that it is still being read and admired.

I don't want to look at the literary quality of these poems or to study them as if for an exam, but I want to draw on what they have to tell us now about God – and that is a great deal. For example, look at poems such as this (which is also sung as a hymn):

My soul, there is a country
Far beyond the stars,
Where stands a winged sentry
All skillful in the wars,
There above noise, and danger
Sweet peace sits crown'd with smiles,
And one born in a manger
Commands the beauteous files,
He is thy gracious friend,
And (O my soul awake!)
Did in pure love descend
To die here for thy sake…

From 'Peace' by Henry Vaughan

When choosing material for the book, I've focused on poems rather than poets, and I've searched for or recalled works that match the Bible readings and the season. So I've surprised myself by omitting many favourites (such as Gerard Manley Hopkins and many current poets) who didn't happen to have written something to fit this purpose. Also, many of us have heard T.S. Eliot and George Herbert quoted in sermons, but I've tried to bring in some others, too. When quoting writers such as W.H. Auden, I'm not trying to judge their life or work as a whole; rather, I want to reflect on their contribution to our spiritual life.

It's fun, too, to claw back some literary figures from simply being monuments of our heritage. Shakespeare, for example, is celebrated as England's great national poet, but of course it's much more important that he wrote astonishingly moving plays. These are works that stir the soul and reflect our lives and hopes now, as much as when they were written 400 years ago. He does write about God and has startling insights into faith. Here, King Lear creates as good a vision of our spiritual life as I've heard, and this is despite the otherwise hopeless circumstances that the king is in by this time in the play:

> *When thou dost ask me blessing, I'll kneel down*
> *And ask of thee forgiveness: so we'll live,*
> *And pray, and sing, and tell old tales, and laugh...*
> *And take upon's the mystery of things*
> *As if we were God's spies...*
>
> *King Lear*, Act 5, Scene 3

I am not bothered about whether we could call these poets 'Christian' in the way we might understand that as a description now. I'm not worried about the detail of their lives, either, but more about the quality of what they wrote, which I think it's fair enough to see in terms of faith. God can speak through all sorts of people, writings and circumstances (as he does in the Bible through figures such as Cyrus the Persian): we can find his word throughout our world.

Some of the arguments in favour of drawing on the witness of poets in this way are like those in favour of using the King James Bible, which I have used for many readings in this book. For the 400th anniversary of the translation in 2011, BRF asked me to gather some short reflections on various passages into a book, *Celebrating the King James Version* (BRF, 2010). When asked to justify using the old version, I found myself saying that it expressed the truths of our faith better and more deeply than some modern translations. This doesn't work for all of it – the epistles can be tough going in the King James Version, for instance – but, alongside newer versions, the old King James has much to offer. It can guide us, right now, in our spiritual lives. And it's the same with poets.

It feels slightly uncomfortable to me to be using these poets – quarrying their work for nuggets of apt quotes, almost as if they were offering Christmas-cracker slogans. Often, I am ripping their lines out of context and depriving their works of the integrity, the wholeness, of the complete text that is an essential part of their life. Certainly I would always rather see a whole play, making sense of its complete story, than a presentation of gems and purple passages from the playwright.

Yet these poems were written to be read. I have enjoyed and benefited from them, and can only recommend and report on what I find. If, by my drawing attention to some small part of these works, anyone is encouraged to read the whole work, so much the better. For it often seems that it is only in poetry that our deepest yearnings can come to the surface. There are so many aspects of God's love for us and ours for him that are hard, if not impossible, to grasp that we can only catch glimpses of part of the picture. The tangential nature of poems – coming at our experience from a particular angle, not feeling they need to record it exhaustively – means that they are ideally placed to convey the complexity, delight and glory of God's care for his creation.

The New Zealand poet James K. Baxter (1926–72) refers to 'an attitude of listening out of which poems may arise… the unheard sound of which poems are translations'. We can make some headway in analysing this attitude but, in the end, it can never be pinned down. God is with us and in us, but also always beyond us. He created us, but he doesn't need us; his creation is pure gift.

Poems, which go beyond a merely literal description of the world, hint at this unknowability, this state of reaching towards infinity. As the French poet Paul Valéry (1871–1945) noted, 'A poem is never finished, only abandoned.' Poets are content to explore and deepen the mystery of God, rather than being obsessed with resolving it. So, for example, several poets whom I quote tease out the paradoxes of Jesus' coming from his heavenly kingdom to be born as a defenceless baby – for instance, John Donne (1572–1631) in 'Annunciation' and 'Nativity': 'Immensity cloistered in thy dear womb' (see the readings for 20 December and Christmas Day). They are not studying this paradox as a problem to be explained so much as a mystery to be revelled in.

Reading poetry

Many people find poems hard or offputting, but I hope that, by quoting mostly short chunks and adding some explanation, I can help to make them more accessible. After all, some of the Bible is written in poetry, such as the Psalms and the Song of Songs, and we would hardly want to stop reading it just because the lines stop short of the right-hand margin of the page.

Sometimes with poems, it's useful to remember that they are written in that particular way not to be difficult or to tease us with some hidden meaning (as if the poet was playing a cruel game with us, the readers). Rather, the poems are set down in verse form as the most exact means of conveying a particular feeling or observation. It can be helpful to try to enjoy the music of the words, at least at first, without attempting to dissect every part of their meaning: let them sink in and play in your head. It's like when you sing a great hymn: you don't expect to grasp it all first time around, but you can repeat its words in your mind. Poetry isn't like a car manual, in which you have to grasp each point before moving on to the next part. And, of course, the words of many hymns are fine poetry.

Advent themes

Advent – the three or four weeks before Christmas – is more than just a preparation for the festive season. It is a distinctive time in the church's year, with its own features, which are a rich blend of different themes. Like Lent, it is a time of penitence, a time to prepare ourselves inwardly for a great festival at its end by reconsidering where we have fallen short. In this respect, it offers a wonderful chance to examine ourselves, to review our lives in a way that we seldom bother to do. We can try to look at ourselves honestly, to probe our sins and repent of them.

It forms a fascinating interplay with the secular calendar. Advent, the beginning of the church's year, is when we look both backwards and forwards – just as the secular world does at its New Year, although it concentrates that mood in the few days around 1 January. But much more than this, the special themes of Advent give it a unique focus, and one that is all too rare for most of us to think about now: death and judgement. The traditional concerns of the four weeks of the season are death, judgement, heaven and hell. This focus also links with the way that, as part of our preparation for the first coming of Jesus at Christmas, churches have traditionally considered its connections with the second coming at the end of time. We look at how the people of God have prepared for Jesus' coming – through the patriarchs and prophets, and on to those directly involved in the events of the nativity: John the Baptist and Mary.

Part of our preparation today involves self-examination and penitence, which are sharpened up by our sense of our ultimate end. No matter that most of us manage to put off all thoughts of the end – usually until death becomes an immediate prospect. This season presents a unique opportunity to think about what ultimately matters. It need not be gloomy: the judgement of God offers redemption for the wrongs we have suffered. In the Old Testament, the poor of Israel look forward to it eagerly, as the time when they will be vindicated. The Advent Bible readings refer to this redemption specifically: for example, Zechariah's song for his son, John the Baptist, says, 'Blessed be the Lord God of Israel; for he hath visited and redeemed his people' (Luke 1:68, KJV: see the reading for Christmas Eve).

During the weeks of Advent, we will be considering these themes but then moving on to ideas about Christmas. Not surprisingly, another part of the point of Advent is to think over Christmas itself, the coming of God into our world – Jesus' becoming one of us and taking on our flesh in the incarnation. The implications of this are staggering, and it should take a lifetime to ponder them. To take just one example, it means that God loves every aspect of our world (as John 3:16 suggests). Jesus entered fully into our humanity; he didn't just visit briefly or dip in his toe. He was not like the Ancient Greek gods who popped down to earth, mainly to cause trouble. Also, we often hear about how incarnational theology should influence our attitude to our planet and to our fellow creatures, human and animal. If God loves the world that he has made, enough to come and be part of it, we too should cherish it and the other creatures in it. So Advent isn't just about our soul and inner peace: we are only one small part of his whole creation, all under the rule of God into eternity.

About this book

The readings are all drawn from the lectionary, the official pattern of Bible passages set down by the Church of England and other churches for their daily worship. This means that we will always be reading verses alongside other Christians, even if we are on our own. It can be very moving to think that thousands of others are pondering the same parts of scripture, as well as to know that the passages have been specially chosen for this day in the year as part of a carefully thought-out plan to cover the most important aspects of our faith.

The book runs all the way through Advent and the beginning of the Christmas season, right up to the Epiphany on 6 January. Its readings can be used in any year, although it was first written with Advent 2012 in mind.

❧ Week 1 ❧

Surveying the territory

This first week of readings begins a long way from Bethlehem, with a range of perspectives from Luke, Matthew, Isaiah and the Psalms. We start by probing some of the biggest questions of our existence, asking (appropriately for Advent, as we saw in the Introduction) about death and God's judgement of us, and about our conflicts and God's peace. God has already answered these restless questions of ours: he loves us enough to have sent his Son at the incarnation (literally, the 'in-fleshment'), when his Son shares in our flesh and blood. This brings together God in heaven with our life that God has created here on earth.

The poet who seems to have much to say about this is T.S. Eliot (1888–1965), the American who came to England as a young man and settled here, finding spiritual roots that he had been searching for. Although he was brought up as a Unitarian, with a mother whose spirituality went deep, he described himself as having been raised 'outside the Christian fold'. He was profoundly moved by seeing such actions (which seem almost routine to some of us) as people kneeling in church. He was attracted by the faith of the Church of England and its Book of Common Prayer, whose 16th-century language mirrors that of writers he admired, such as Shakespeare, George Herbert and Lancelot Andrewes. He treasured aspects of faith that, I must admit, I often take for granted.

For this week's readings, I have drawn on T.S. Eliot's poetry to examine these big questions of existence, in poems such as *The Waste Land* (1922), which shows a deep understanding of the malaise of the modern world. Crucially, though, Eliot doesn't leave it at that; he also points towards answers to our modern alienation. He is not afraid to argue that it is God who created us to love him and who alone can satisfy us. So, in *The Dry Salvages* (1941), he writes of the gift of moments when we sense God more deeply. This leads on to the most marvellous gift of all, the coming of Jesus.

1 December

Luke 21:29–36 (NRSV)

Praying for strength to face the questions

Then he told them a parable: 'Look at the fig tree and all the trees; as soon as they sprout leaves you can see for yourselves and know that summer is already near. So also, when you see these things taking place, you know that the kingdom of God is near. Truly I tell you, this generation will not pass away until all things have taken place. Heaven and earth will pass away, but my words will not pass away. Be on guard so that your hearts are not weighed down with dissipation and drunkenness and the worries of this life, and that day does not catch you unexpectedly, like a trap. For it will come upon all who live on the face of the whole earth. Be alert at all times, praying that you may have the strength to escape all these things that will take place, and to stand before the Son of Man.'

As we enter Advent, the preparation for Christmas, with its themes of judgement – indeed, its serious ideas of death, judgement, heaven and hell – we might pause for a while to think why all this is so important. The matter in hand isn't just about some slight improvement to the quality of our life or something that will cheer us up for a while. No, this is absolutely fundamental to our existence. These are the biggest questions of all. We have to recognise that we need to be rescued.

The business of God's coming to be with us and in us – each one of us – is at the centre of our lives. This is the 'still point of the turning world' (as T.S. Eliot put it in *Burnt Norton*, 1935), the reason why people change the course of their living and try to model themselves on the God who comes to us in Jesus of Nazareth. We need to join in the prayer for strength at the end of this passage, so that we can be ready when God comes.

He is not a god like the one imagined by some atheists, who leaves the world to its own devices, and us all alone on a desolate plain – as Matthew Arnold (1822–88) famously describes it in his poem 'Dover Beach':

And we are here as on a darkling plain
Swept with confused alarms of struggle and flight,
Where ignorant armies clash by night.

No, this is a God who comes to live with us and to mingle his existence with ours. So, as we struggle to get our heads round these ideas, the season of Advent offers us a wonderful opportunity in its rich mix of themes: darkness and light; judgement and vindication; expectation, hope and fulfilment. It's a chance to work out why we are here and to search for the God who loves us into being.

We begin by turning to God, praying for his strength to help us, so that we might avoid the 'dissipation' and 'worries of this life' (Luke 21:34). As I mentioned in the Introduction, we can also draw on the witness of fellow pilgrims, such as T.S. Eliot, who have also looked at these big questions. Much of Eliot's writing deals with Advent themes, such as death, judgement and purgation. Even before he became a Christian at the end of his 30s, he dwelt on these subjects. Thus, in *The Waste Land* (published in 1922, several years before he officially joined the Church of England), he famously writes of the crowd of workers in the 'Unreal city': 'so many, / I had not thought death had undone so many.' He vividly portrays the spiritual emptiness of Western Europe (particularly London), in the aftermath of World War I:

I think we are in rats' alley
Where the dead men lost their bones…

'Are you alive, or not? Is there nothing in your head?'

Later, he describes people as being 'each in his prison'. Eliot certainly captures the 'dissipation and drunkenness and the worries of this life' that Jesus warns us about. If anything, these dissipations have got worse nearly a century later, as technology has artificially speeded everything up and the internet offers all kinds of temptations, despite the many positive ways it enables us to communicate. We seem increasingly to have 'strained time-ridden faces / Distracted from distraction by distraction', as Eliot wrote in *Burnt Norton*.

In this welter of perversity and debasement, we need all the more to turn to God, praying for strength in the way of Luke 21:36. It seems bizarre that the stresses of today's world don't drive more people to God, when they can't fail to be aware of the big questions – including those Advent themes of death and judgement – even if they strenuously ignore them. Perhaps it is simply that Jesus' warnings in this passage are always needed, as each new generation finds a way of wriggling out of thinking about them. Throughout this book, we'll try to face them, to prepare for the coming of God, praying for his strength to help us face the big questions, which we know are there but which we are always reluctant to look at honestly.

For reflection

I give thanks to my God always for you because of the grace of God that has been given you in Christ Jesus… so that you are not lacking in any spiritual gift as you wait for the revealing of our Lord Jesus Christ. He will also strengthen you to the end, so that you may be blameless on the day of our Lord Jesus Christ.

1 CORINTHIANS 1:4, 7–8

2 December

Luke 21:20, 23b–28 (NRSV)

The mystery of the end of the world

'When you see Jerusalem surrounded by armies, then know that its desolation has come near... For there will be great distress on the earth and wrath against this people; they will fall by the edge of the sword and be taken away as captives among all nations; and Jerusalem will be trampled on by the Gentiles, until the times of the Gentiles are fulfilled. There will be signs in the sun, the moon, and the stars, and on the earth distress among nations confused by the roaring of the sea and the waves. People will faint from fear and foreboding of what is coming upon the world, for the powers of the heavens will be shaken. Then they will see "the Son of Man coming in a cloud" with power and great glory. Now when these things begin to take place, stand up and raise your heads, because your redemption is drawing near.'

This passage comes immediately before the one we read yesterday. Here, Jesus tells of the judgement to come. I must admit, there is much here that makes me uncomfortable – and in a way that doesn't have much to do with the second coming or being judged by God. For these verses (and similar ones in the gospels, such as those in Mark 13) are ones that I associate with all sorts of religious zealots – people shouting on street corners or on the internet about the end of the world or gathering in American deserts to wait for the rapture. It all seems wrong: misguided, unhelpful and tainting all religious people with a hint of freakishness and gullibility. It is like what G.K. Chesterton said: 'When people stop believing in God, they don't believe in nothing – they believe in anything.'

T.S. Eliot nails these people when he writes in *The Dry Salvages* about those who seek to:

>   … *release omens*
>   *By sortilege, or tea leaves, riddle the inevitable*
>   *With playing cards, fiddle with pentagrams…*
>   *To explore the womb, or tomb, or dreams; all these*
>   *are usual*
>   *Pastimes and drugs, and features of the press:*
>   *And always will be.*

Yet here are these passages about the end of the world, in the New Testament, coming from Jesus. This is scripture, so, like his difficult sayings and the cruellest parts of the Psalms, we can't just sweep it under the carpet. The second coming is a central part of Advent: as we wait for Jesus' first coming at Christmas, we think of his later coming at the end of time.

One approach to all this, not surprisingly, might be again to remind ourselves what the point is: God is coming in order to judge us. Yes, we have all sinned and fallen short of the glory of God (Romans 3:23; 1 John 1:8–9). We have been cruel or selfish. T.S. Eliot writes about this in *Little Gidding* (1942) in a way that sends shivers down the spine, especially when we are haunted by the clinging memories of the mistakes we have made:

> *And last, the rending pain of re-enactment*
> *Of all that you have done, and been; the shame*
> *Of motives late revealed, and the awareness*
> *Of things ill-done and done to others' harm*
> *Which once you took for exercise of virtue.*
> *Then fools' approval stings, and honour stains.*

Often we do need to reflect on our past actions and attitudes. But, when we have done this wholeheartedly, we then need to move on: to repent of our sins, to put right as much as we possibly can, and to set it all in the context of what we know about God's love. As W.H. Auden (1907–73) writes, in *For the Time Being* (1944), 'Let us be contrite without anxiety.' We know that we have a fair, wise and compassionate judge, who understands from the inside what it is to be human. 'For we do not have a high priest who is unable to sympathise with our weaknesses, but we have one who in every respect has been tested as we are, yet without sin' (Hebrews 4:15).

We may have done terrible things but, amazingly, God has forgiven us. In the end, there is no need to fear or to apply Bible passages such as this one from Luke 21 in the way that some extremists do (especially the ones who assume that they themselves are saved, while everyone else is doomed). We realise that God will judge the world, but we cannot really know the details of the 'great distress' mentioned here. In whatever way it happens, though, the main point of this passage is our response. Jesus tells us, 'Stand up and raise your heads, because your redemption is drawing near' (v. 28). If we have really been wronged, and we approach our Father in heaven in honesty and contrition, God's judgement will vindicate us. Most of us struggle to take this in: we cannot believe how God can be so good to us, and we can become trapped in fear.

For reflection

> *He does not deal with us according to our sins,*
> *   nor repay us according to our iniquities.*
> *For as the heavens are high above the earth,*
> *   so great is his steadfast love towards those who*
> *   fear him;*
> *as far as the east is from the west,*
> *   so far he removes our transgressions from us.*
> PSALM 103:10–12

Take a few minutes to ponder these words, especially verse 12. Try reading them two or three times, and let them sink into your mind and heart.

3 December

Isaiah 2:2–5 (KJV, abridged)

Turning swords into ploughshares

And it shall come to pass in the last days, that the mountain of the Lord's house shall be established in the top of the mountains… And many people shall go and say, Come ye, and let us go up to the mountain of the Lord, to the house of the God of Jacob; and he will teach us of his ways, and we will walk in his paths… And he shall judge among the nations, and shall rebuke many people: and they shall beat their swords into plowshares, and their spears into pruninghooks: nation shall not lift up sword against nation, neither shall they learn war any more. O house of Jacob, come ye, and let us walk in the light of the Lord.

I am using the King James Version here because it conveys more than most modern translations do and – in this passage at least – really isn't hard to understand. It suggests more of the poetry of the words, which is an essential part of their meaning, and one that other versions lose.

This is not a straightforward report but a prophecy of the future, a vision of what could happen. These are the sorts of words that can keep us going through the tough times and the boring times and the times when we feel we've no idea whether we're doing the right thing or not.

This is a central part of the Advent experience. The season takes us down into the darkness of death, just as (in the northern hemisphere, at least) the days are getting shorter and colder and the hours of darkness are getting longer. In the middle of these shadows, we are urged to wait on God and ponder what his coming will bring. So we need to know that God 'shall judge among the nations, and shall rebuke many people' (v. 4). We might want to be reassured on this point, as we can see that the wicked seem to be prospering as usual.

It is the depth of this longing for peace and justice that T.S. Eliot plumbs throughout *The Waste Land*. As we have seen over the past two days, he holds up a mirror to a society ravaged by conflict, in terms of both warfare and turmoil between people and within individuals. Although he was deemed medically unfit to fight, Eliot experienced the aftermath of the trauma of World War I (he was keen to volunteer for combat). For many of the soldiers, and those left at home, these famous words from Isaiah became a focus for their dearest hopes. During and after the fighting, they clung on to the hope that this was a war to end all wars, and that 'nation shall not lift up sword against nation, neither shall they learn war any more' (v. 4). Famously, the war was meant to be 'all over by Christmas', as if that miraculous time of year would bring an end to strife and return everyone home to their families. Of course, it didn't happen like that, but people were surely right not to lose hope, so that when that Christmas did come at last – in 1918 – they could focus on the coming of Jesus as a vulnerable baby, as an answer to the horrors of killing.

Eliot's thinking and work moved on from the bleakness of *The Waste Land* – though it was not a simple progression to the broad sunlit uplands of faith. I've heard whole lectures describing him as the poet of 'between': torn between various possibilities and constantly in tension. Certainly, 'between' is a crucial word in his poetry and he often seeks a resolution – for example, at the end of *Ash Wednesday*, a long poem that he wrote in 1930, when he had been a Christian for several years. As we shall see in a couple of days' time, this resolution involves a quest for true peace and wholeness in 'the time of tension between dying and birth', as he prays, 'Suffer me not to be separated.' His prayer seems to spring from his fear of loneliness and of being without God.

In speaking to this desire for peace and wholeness, today's passage from Isaiah ends, crucially, with an invitation: 'O house of Jacob, come ye, and let us walk in the light of the Lord.' Just as, a few verses earlier, the people had been asked to go to God's mountain and his house, in order to learn his ways, this suggests that there is always something we can do about a situation, always a response we can make. The situation may be truly bleak – whether it involves a war, a smaller conflict between people we love, or even the struggles within our own hearts – but God will judge and bring peace. And we can play our part. Swords will be beaten into ploughshares: the resources that we had made into weapons will become part of the means to nourish us. The energy that we put into conflict can be redirected to building up wholeness. We can all make our own attempt, however small, to walk in the light of the Lord, by trusting him in prayer, worship, thought and action.

Even at the end of *The Waste Land*, after all the desolation, Eliot ends by invoking peace. His finishes the long poem with the phrase 'Shantih shantih shantih', which, he says in his accompanying notes, is 'a formal ending to an Upanishad [part of the Hindu scriptures]. "The Peace which passeth understanding" is our equivalent to this word.'

For reflection

Can you think of any situations closer to home – in your own heart or between people who are dear to you – where you might help to beat swords into ploughshares, so that we can all turn our gifts to growing rather than fighting?

4 December

Isaiah 11:1–2, 4, 6, 8–9 (KJV)

Living up to the hope

And there shall come forth a rod out of the stem of Jesse, and a Branch shall grow out of his roots: And the spirit of the Lord shall rest upon him, the spirit of wisdom and understanding, the spirit of counsel and might, the spirit of knowledge and of the fear of the Lord... But with righteousness shall he judge the poor, and reprove with equity for the meek of the earth: and he shall smite the earth with the rod of his mouth, and with the breath of his lips shall he slay the wicked... The wolf also shall dwell with the lamb, and the leopard shall lie down with the kid; and the calf and the young lion and the fatling together; and a little child shall lead them... And the sucking child shall play on the hole of the asp, and the weaned child shall put his hand on the cockatrice den. They shall not hurt nor destroy in all my holy mountain: for the earth shall be full of the knowledge of the Lord, as the waters cover the sea.

Some chapters later than yesterday's reading, but still in the first part of the book of Isaiah, here is another celebrated passage, another central Advent text, looking forward to the coming of the Saviour. This figure will be a wise judge who will be both fair and holy. His presence will bring in what seems to be an era of other-worldly harmony, as nature 'red in tooth and claw' is tamed and the whole earth 'shall be full of the knowledge of the Lord, as the waters cover the sea' (v. 9). As we heard in earlier passages, there is no need to be afraid.

Again, this is a vision of supernatural peace: more than an absence of conflict, it is the deep peace 'that passeth understanding' and is not as the world gives: 'Peace I leave with you; my peace I give to you. I do not give to you as the world gives. Do not let your hearts be troubled, and do not let them be afraid' (John 14:27, NRSV). This is much more than a cheerful optimism that things will probably turn out all right. Rather, it is a solid hope about how the world could be, under God's rule.

It's a sweeping generalisation, but Americans seem to be better at this type of hope than British people and other Europeans (and I'd put other nationalities such as Australians, New Zealanders and Canadians with the US on this one). There's something about tired old cynical Europe that seems to create more hurdles in our mind to the idea that things might actually get better. You only have to recall President Obama's election campaign in 2008, when he and his supporters specifically utilised this sense of hope, in order to encourage people to take action and vote for him. There was much talk of 'Obama hope' and 'Yes, we can.' So, in this respect at least, T.S. Eliot is drawing on his American heritage rather than the spiritual desert that he found on the opposite side of the Atlantic – as he writes in *Little Gidding*, 'when I left my body on a distant shore'.

As you might expect from someone who laid hold of this sustaining vision by publicly declaring his faith, Eliot is able to build on the faint hints at the end of *The Waste Land* towards fuller realisations of Christian hope in his later poetry, after his baptism. So, when he comes to *Journey of the Magi* (1927), he is, among many other things, weighing up hopes, fears and expectations as he tells of the wise men who travelled to find the Christ-child.

> ... *were we led all that way for*
> *Birth or Death?...*
>   *I had seen birth and death,*
> *But had thought they were different; this Birth was*
> *Hard and bitter agony for us, like Death, our death.*
> *We return to our places, these Kingdoms,*

But no longer at ease here, in the old dispensation,
With an alien people clutching their gods.
I should be glad of another death.

After they had seen the vision and its fulfilment, the wise men had a new perspective on what mattered. They had died to their old ideas and the things that used to satisfy them; and a new and more definite hope had been born within them, so that they were no longer content with the old ways.

This is the hope for the coming Saviour, not just that everything is vaguely going to be all right because of the general virtues of wisdom and understanding (Isaiah 11:2), but specifically that the poor and meek will be judged fairly (vv. 4–5). So there will be justice in places such as Congo, Darfur, Israel and Palestine, Afghanistan and elsewhere, and for people everywhere who have been weighed down by pain. Those who have suffered so horribly will be vindicated. It is only the wicked who should be afraid.

For reflection

Think what a difference it would make if more of us were truly convinced of this sure ground for hope in the everyday details of our lives. Is there anything that you are anxious about today that you need to offer up to God, in the knowledge that he will judge fairly? Can you trust his judgement in the spirit of knowing that he is coming to rule justly?

5 December

Psalm 23 (trans. Joseph Addison, 1712)

Looking death in the face

The Lord my pasture shall prepare
and feed me with a shepherd's care;
his presence shall my wants supply
and guard me with a watchful eye;
my noonday walks he shall attend
and all my midnight hours defend.

When in the sultry glebe I faint
or on the thirsty mountain pant,
to fertile vales and dewy meads
my weary wandering steps he leads,
where peaceful rivers, soft and slow,
amid the verdant landscape flow.

Though in a bare and rugged way
through devious lonely wilds I stray,
thy bounty shall my pains beguile;
the barren wilderness shall smile
with sudden greens and herbage crowned,
and streams shall murmur all around.

Though in the paths of death I tread,
with gloomy horrors overspread,
my steadfast heart shall fear no ill,
for thou, O Lord, art with me still;
thy friendly crook shall give me aid,
and guide me through the dreadful shade.

This is a version of the most celebrated psalm of all, Psalm 23, by the poet Joseph Addison (1672–1719). It might sound more poetic than most versions (I especially like 'sultry glebe' and 'thirsty mountain pant'), but it is recognisably the same Bible passage. It is still found in hymn books such as *The New English Hymnal* and *Hymns Ancient & Modern New Standard*. For me, it offers a way of making the familiar ideas of Psalm 23 come through in a fresh way. This seems particularly important when considering one of the central themes of Advent: death.

There are times when, despite our knowledge of the rock on which our faith is founded, and the blessing of realising that God has triumphed ultimately, there are still dark valleys through which we must travel. There is no other way. We can't escape death – and our own death comes after we have experienced many deaths and other losses around us.

Advent is one of the times in the church's year when we are encouraged to consider this. It's a precious opportunity, which I think we should seize. One of the things I've been particularly struck by, since I was treated for breast cancer a year or so ago, is the way we are so extremely reluctant to think about death. Of course, this is only natural, but (perhaps short-sightedly) I hadn't realised that it went so very deep. Even if the outlook is bleak and we are told that our chances aren't great, we still don't quite believe it. It seems that it's only at a very late stage, when we're confronted with the fact that death is near, that we really take it in.

This reluctance seems to be different from the vague and sometimes paralysing fear that many people have of cancer, assuming that any such diagnosis is a death sentence rather than something from which most people recover. The key to it, for me, is the uncertainty of those fears: they can't be pinned down, so they expand, loom large and find their way into all the crevices of our minds. When we have something more specific to deal with, such as medical information about our health, we can isolate it and focus on it realistically so that it doesn't take on undue importance.

Advent offers a chance to look truthfully at death and to allay our fears. If we cannot do this, we risk cowering under the shadow of all sorts of imaginary terrors (the 'gloomy horrors' and 'dreadful shade' of Addison's translation of the psalm). The message from God in this psalm is that, yes, we will go through the valley of the shadow of death at some time – we cannot avoid it – but we can be certain that God will always be with us.

I think this is part of what T.S. Eliot is suggesting in *Ash Wednesday*, but then he takes us to another place as well. In the midst of our anxieties (the 'time of tension', see below) and loneliness – where perhaps we worry about our own and our children's future, or we might fear that we will have to cope with shapeless terrors on our own or that everything is going to fall apart (we will 'be separated', as Eliot puts it) – it is here that we need actively to seek God. We need to sit still and look for his will for our situation. We can do this by offering our cares and needs to God in prayer and worship, and by trying to think what wisdom from the Bible and God's teaching can speak to our fears. One way is to repeat, aloud or in our head, a powerful phrase, such as 'I will not leave you comfortless' (John 14:18, KJV) or 'My grace is sufficient' (2 Corinthians 12:9, NRSV).

In the following lines, Eliot prays that God might help us to see truthfully (not 'mock ourselves with falsehood') and to seek his will.

This is the time of tension between dying and birth
The place of solitude...
Suffer us not to mock ourselves with falsehood
Teach us to care and not to care
Teach us to sit still
Even among these rocks,
Our peace in His will...
Suffer me not to be separated

And let my cry come unto Thee.

For reflection

Do you have any fears for your future that you could try to examine specifically and honestly, setting them before God today?

6 December

Matthew 7:21, 24–27 (NRSV)

Be surprised by joy

[Jesus said to his disciples,] 'Not everyone who says to me, "Lord, Lord", will enter the kingdom of heaven, but only one who does the will of my Father in heaven... Everyone then who hears these words of mine and acts on them will be like a wise man who built his house on rock. The rain fell, the floods came, and the winds blew and beat on that house, but it did not fall, because it had been founded on rock. And everyone who hears these words of mine and does not act on them will be like a foolish man who built his house on sand. The rain fell, and the floods came, and the winds blew and beat against that house, and it fell – and great was its fall!'

I can't read this passage without thinking of the old Sunday school song 'The wise man built his house upon the rock'. I can still remember the actions, especially for the lines 'The rain came down and the floods came up.' It's such a good story, and the house built on sand is such a vivid image that it is still used to describe ill-founded plans by people who never open a Bible.

Yet it seems interesting to look at the parable together with some of the verses immediately before it (see v. 21, quoted above), which give it a whole new dimension. It's not just about building on the rock of God, basing our life on his commandments. It's also about the difference between only hearing the words of Jesus – merely being one who knows the name of the Lord and cries it out – and actually doing God's will. We all know that there is often a yawning gulf between the two. We can be familiar with Christian teaching and can believe that we are calling on the Lord, but we can be a long way from truly carrying out that teaching and feeling the security of the rock beneath our feet.

Isn't this a tediously familiar lesson? Christians are always being accused of hypocrisy, of wanting to seem religious while really being spiteful and selfish. It's what many of our critics seem to assume. They might grant that there are one or two genuinely holy people (perhaps supposedly harmless old ladies in the pews at the back of church), but still believe that most of the others who go to church do so because they think they're better than anyone else, that they're smug and disapproving of others while fancying themselves as devout.

This seems such a tired old cliché to the rest of us that it's hard to know where to start in contradicting it. Of course, we should try to be as truthful as we can in our Christian lives and to focus on God's will more, rather than wondering how we might appear to others. Sometimes we can be almost too self-effacing about this, hiding our lights under bushels for fear of being misunderstood or seeming pious. I guess the solution is some sort of happy medium, whereby we try to put Jesus' words into practice with as much integrity as we can muster while working out in our own mind what we can say when religious subjects crop up in conversation with others (as they always seem to do eventually).

On that central accusation of thinking ourselves superior to others, we might reflect on the fact that we are all sinners, praying, 'Forgive us our trespasses, as we forgive those who trespass against us', as Jesus recommends in Matthew 6:12, 14–15. When he refers to 'these words of mine' (7:24), he might mean the words he has just spoken in the sermon on the mount (Matthew 5—7), so that's a good place to begin when looking at the teaching we want to follow. Those chapters present a striking picture of the kingdom of God as a reversal of the ways of the world. In the Beatitudes, for example (Matthew 5:3–12), the usual order of life is turned on its head as the meek and the mourners, rather than the successful and happy people, are called 'blessed'.

When it comes to acting on Jesus' words and trying to 'work out your own salvation with fear and trembling' (Philippians 2:12), most of the time we can only carry on in hope, with the occasional vision of God's love. Just occasionally, very rarely, we are given a glimpse of his glory. C.S. Lewis describes such times, in his autobiography *Surprised by Joy* (1955), in terms of sublime experiences of the transcendent – the sense of desire and delight that he calls Joy. T.S. Eliot puts it like this in *The Dry Salvages*:

> *For most of us, there is only the unattended*
> *Moment, the moment in and out of time,*
> *The distraction fit, lost in a shaft of sunlight…*
> *   … These are only hints and guesses,*
> *Hints followed by guesses; and the rest*
> *Is prayer, observance, discipline, thought and action.*

Those five words, 'prayer, observance, discipline, thought and action', summarise what I believe it means to act on God's word. This is what we can all get on with doing, right now – never mind what others think.

For reflection

Have you ever had what you felt was a glimpse of God's glory? If so, in what ways have you been able to build on it in your everyday life?

7 December

Psalm 27:1–2, 5, 9–10, 12, 15
(BCP/Coverdale, abridged)

Incarnation: the impossible but actual union

The Lord is my light and my salvation; whom then shall I fear: the Lord is the strength of my life; of whom then shall I be afraid? When the wicked, even mine enemies and my foes, came upon me to eat up my flesh: they stumbled and fell... For in the time of trouble he shall hide me in his tabernacle: yea, in the secret place of his dwelling shall he hide me, and set me up upon a rock of stone... My heart hath talked of thee, Seek ye my face: Thy face, Lord, will I seek. O hide not thou thy face from me: nor cast thy servant away in displeasure... When my father and my mother forsake me: the Lord taketh me up... I should utterly have fainted: but that I believe verily to see the goodness of the Lord in the land of the living.

At the end of this first week of readings, we return to a psalm. I find this one irresistible and inspiring, and I can see why it was chosen for Advent. It draws on some of the themes of Psalm 23, which we read two days ago – about the comforting presence of God – but takes them further. So there is a deep sense of the inner strength that God gives us amid a vividly described fear of the menace of enemies. These terrors are more immediately threatening – they want to devour me, and are like a besieging army – but, against them, God is all the mightier. He is 'the strength of my life' (v. 1).

Psalm 27 gains much of its power from the ease with which we can translate its general talk of fears and enemies to our own individual circumstances. We might imagine the 'enemies' as besetting sins, debilitating anxieties, cancerous cells, people who have let us down, or whatever else seems to eat us up. In the face of all this, we are encouraged to look for the Lord, who has helped us in the past and will uphold us again. We have some natural instinct to search out God ('My heart hath talked of thee, Seek ye my face': v. 9a), but we need to make some effort to act on it ('Thy face, Lord, will I seek': v. 9b). In a way, this plays out what we read yesterday about hearing and then doing the will of the Lord. There is something for us to do: it is not just about passive acceptance or waiting. And the rewards are wonderful – solid and reliable: 'He shall hide me in his tabernacle: yea, in the secret place of his dwelling shall he hide me, and set me up upon a rock of stone' (v. 5).

Yet this is not merely a reward for good behaviour, as if God were like a sugar daddy, doling out rewards and punishments – as some people imagine. Instead, it comes from a much deeper relationship: one of trust, commitment and, most importantly, love. That is what 'my light and my salvation' (v. 1) and the tender picture of God's hiding me 'in the secret place of his dwelling' (v. 5) suggest to me. We are held in the shepherd's arms, close to his heart.

What does this salvation consist of? Developing yesterday's 'prayer, observance, discipline, thought and action', the very next lines in *The Dry Salvages* are:

> *The hint half guessed, the gift half understood, is*
> *   Incarnation.*
> *Here the impossible union*
> *Of spheres of existence is actual,*
> *Here the past and future*
> *Are conquered, and reconciled...*

So the light, salvation and lovingkindness that God offers us are not distant, abstract ideas: they are embodied in a person, God's Son, Jesus Christ. We're not left on our own to struggle and muddle through prayer, observance and the rest – because we have Jesus, who has come to stand alongside us. God knows now from the inside what it is like to be human: he has reconciled heaven and earth in what might seem to be an 'impossible union'.

This is one of the reasons why Christianity isn't about being nice and good and a decent chap. It is much more fundamental than that, being bound up with the reason why we were created as sentient beings. Also, it does not depend on our own efforts. It's about being saved by the God who came to be among us, who is 'the strength of my life'. He is both within and around us.

For reflection

Try to think of one 'enemy' that you can confront today with the strength of your life – God, who is with us, both within and beyond us.

> Likewise the Spirit helps us in our weakness; for we do not know how to pray as we ought, but that very Spirit intercedes with sighs too deep for words. And God, who searches the heart, knows what is the mind of the Spirit, because the Spirit intercedes for the saints according to the will of God. We know that all things work together for good for those who love God, who are called according to his purpose.
> ROMANS 8:26–28

❦ Week 2 ❦

The untwisted path

In this second week of Advent, we're again drawing on the readings set by the church for its daily services, using mainly the Old Testament passages. These highlight the Advent themes of being not only purified but also comforted by God. So we can look ahead to God's coming at Christmas to purge our sins as well as his coming alongside us, in love, to save us.

One of the poets whose work seems to capture these themes well is Alfred, Lord Tennyson (1809–92). He might be thought of as a grand old Victorian – a brooding, bearded figure – but his poetry explores the depths of bereavement experienced in youth. As we shall see on 9 December, he is also taken as a textbook example of Victorian Doubt (with a capital 'D') in a rather dreary way, in the context of arguments about atheism – again, suggesting an air of heavy velvet curtains and dusty stuffed animals under glass domes. But really his poems can thrill us with their musical rhythms, touching beauty and rare ability to probe our questioning.

8 December

Psalm 146:1–6, 9–10 (BCP/Coverdale)

Not with the hope of gaining

Praise the Lord, O my soul; while I live will I praise the Lord: yea, as long as I have any being, I will sing praises unto my God. O put not your trust in princes, nor in any child of man: for there is no help in them. For when the breath of man goeth forth he shall turn again to his earth: and then all his thoughts perish. Blessed is he that hath the God of Jacob for his help: and whose hope is in the Lord his God; Who made heaven and earth, the sea, and all that therein is: who keepeth his promise for ever; Who helpeth them to right that suffer wrong: who feedeth the hungry… The Lord careth for the strangers, he defendeth the fatherless and widow: as for the way of the ungodly, he turneth it upside down. The Lord thy God, O Sion, shall be King forevermore: and throughout all generations.

I am using the old translation here, as the meaning seems fairly clear, if you can avoid being put off by the -eth endings. Only in verse 4 ('For when the breath of man goeth forth…') might some explanation be helpful. The NRSV translates it, 'When their breath departs, they return to the earth; on that very day their plans perish.' But generally the poetic qualities make it a fuller, more rounded version of what is, after all, poetry.

This passage leads on from what we found last week, on 4 December, about God's vindication of those who have suffered. We shouldn't be terrified of his judgement. Yes, we are all sinners, but God is merciful and loves us as his children. He will put things right if we have been unfairly treated. He is the only one who sees the full picture. As we say at the beginning of the Holy Communion service, God is the one 'to whom all hearts are open, all desires known, and from whom no secrets are hidden', which means that he is the only one who can ultimately comfort us.

This belief can be twisted into a highly coloured image of the oppressed poor dreaming of 'pie in the sky when they die', or even of putting up with all sorts of injustice because of the promise of redemption. Atheists and critics of religion love this image of religious people as gullible, other-worldly and concerned only with a personal salvation that ignores the real suffering in this world. The playwright David Hare says about Christians:

> I suppose I cannot help believing agnostics
> live a life which is tougher and in some sense

nobler than yours. Whatever your sincere
mutterings about your own shortcomings, the
fact is, all your money is not on this race. You
have a side-bet... For you, everything will one
day be put right. For us, we must work to make
it right now.

David Hare, *Via Dolorosa & When Shall We Live?* (Faber, 1998)

I think David Hare is profoundly wrong here. Like others
who have argued in similar ways, he doesn't seem to
understand that this world matters to Christians much
more than the next one does. We are called to care for the
people and the rest of creation that God loves, and not
to be motivated by a self-interested desire for our own
comfort in the future. Anyone who honestly follows the
Lord in the way of the cross, the Lord who came to serve
and not to be served, is transformed into Christlikeness
(Matthew 20:26–28). Those who want to save their life
will lose it (16:24–26). The transformation is incomplete
and we're still sinners, but we are a long way from being
the sort of people who ignore the problems of this world,
with our eye on the main chance in heaven.

What this line of criticism fails to grasp (among other
things) is that the Christian faith is a continuing relationship with our Father, more than a set of beliefs that we
act upon. It's not an ideology or line of policy that we put

into practice (like a company carrying out its business using a particular way of thinking); rather, it's a relationship with the God who has given himself for us and made the ultimate sacrifice to save us. He loved us first, and we respond in love for him.

So when we read in this psalm, 'O put not your trust in princes' (v. 2), it is more than a clear-eyed warning about the dangers of secular rulers (which in itself raises bitter, vigorous nods of approval from most of us), and more even than a promise that God will be more faithful to us than our fellow humans will. It is a call to sort out our priorities and see where our deepest loyalty and hopes should be focused. This is the Lord who made heaven and earth, and who will keep faith with us (v. 5). He calls us to place our hopes in him and to love him.

For reflection

I love thee, Lord, but not because
I hope for heaven thereby,
nor yet for fear that loving not
I might for ever die;
but for that thou didst all the world
upon the cross embrace…

Then why, most loving Jesus Christ,
should I not love thee well,
not for the sake of winning heaven,
nor any fear of hell;

not with the hope of gaining aught,
nor seeking a reward;
but as thyself hast loved me,
O ever loving Lord!

Spanish, 17th century; trans. Edward Caswall (1814–78);
adapt. Percy Dearmer (1867–1936)

9 December

Malachi 3:1–4 (KJV, abridged)

Is good the final goal of ill?

Behold, I will send my messenger, and he shall prepare the way before me: and the Lord, whom ye seek, shall suddenly come to his temple, even the messenger of the covenant… But who may abide the day of his coming? and who shall stand when he appeareth? for he is like a refiner's fire, and like fullers' soap: And he shall sit as a refiner and purifier of silver: and he shall purify the sons of Levi, and purge them as gold and silver, that they may offer unto the Lord an offering in righteousness. Then shall the offering of Judah and Jerusalem be pleasant unto the Lord, as in the days of old, and as in former years.

This passage continues from yesterday's reading in focusing on the Advent theme of judgement and the Lord's vindication of those who have suffered. It is familiar to many of us from the words set to music by Handel in *Messiah*: 'But who may abide the day of his coming?' I can't read the words without thinking of the thrilling quick notes of the violins on 'For he is like a refiner's fire', which seem to dart around as if looking for an escape from the coming trial.

Messiah was first performed during Lent and includes many elements suitable for that season, but nowadays it has become more associated with Christmas, perhaps partly thanks to its use of passages such as this one. It focuses on a key Advent theme, reminding us again that the season isn't just about preparation for the stable at Bethlehem but searches deeper, probing exactly why Jesus came to earth. Crucially, it links the Lord's coming to his judgement of us. It's not only a case of his coming alongside us to share in our humanity: he is coming to examine us. And who can stand when he appears? None of us, of course. But God does not leave us in our sins; he returns to us, so that we may return to him and make our offerings (v. 4). This is the interplay of justice – the judgement we deserve for our sins – and mercy – God's lovingkindness towards us – that we see throughout the Old and New Testaments.

Many poets have dramatised the interplay tellingly, but I would like to focus on one, now and over the next few days, whom we don't always link to Christian faith: Alfred, Lord Tennyson. He is often quoted in intellectual discussions of the Victorian mind and religious doubt, as if he were a philosopher in verse, so the lines that get endlessly wheeled out are 'For there's more faith in honest doubt, / Believe me, than in half the creeds', from *In Memoriam* (1850). But my affection for him stems from the way his reflections always came back to the personal; they weren't academic definitions but expressions of desperate searching, to make sense of the most influential experience of his life, which was the death of his closest friend, Arthur Hallam, when they were both in their early 20s. We see this most clearly in *In Memoriam*, the long poem that he published nearly 20 years after his bereavement, but also in other works, such as '*Morte d'Arthur*' and *Ulysses*, which he began soon after he heard the news of the death.

I must confess that I'm rather fed up with hearing about 'honest doubt', which seems to be quoted more by those who want to seek an intellectual ballast for their own reluctance to understand faith than by those who have searched with rigour and integrity and still find it genuinely hard to believe, even when they wish they did. The latter group does exist, but we seem to hear much more from those who just don't like the idea of religion and don't show any evidence of knowing much about it. That may be uncharitable, when we are called to love our enemies (Luke 6:27), but I don't believe that Tennyson can be drawn into the argument so simply.

Here, however, I am reflecting only on some of the aspects of faith that he brings alive. In this vein, Tennyson struggles with the idea of purification and God's bringing good from suffering. He writes of how tough this seems in the heat of anguish. Here is genuine 'honest doubt', not disengaged intellectual posturing:

Oh yet we trust that somehow good
  Will be the final goal of ill…

  I can but trust that good shall fall
  At last – far off – at last, to all,
And every winter change to spring.

So runs my dream: but what am I?
  An infant crying in the night:
  An infant crying for the light:
And with no language but a cry.

Tennyson, with this image of inner torment, is like the psalmist who says, 'All the night make I my bed to swim; I water my couch with my tears' (Psalm 6:6, KJV). By the very end of the poem, he appeals to what he later described as 'Free-will in man' to 'Flow thro' our deeds and make them pure'. He can write in his Epilogue that he has 'grown / To something greater than before', but this is tentative. He does not relish the anguish of the learning process, despite the most famous lines of the poem:

> 'Tis better to have loved and lost
> Than never to have loved at all.

For reflection

Do you agree with Tennyson's celebrated lines that it is 'better to have loved and lost…'? He seems to cling to this conclusion, after much wrestling with doubt. Such a hope is all that he is left with, perhaps sensing the nature of love as a gift from God. But do you sometimes suspect that it might be best not to be disturbed by such a gift as love?

10 December

Isaiah 35:1–6, 8, 10 (NRSV, abridged)

The vision that sustains

The wilderness and the dry land shall be glad, the desert shall rejoice and blossom... They shall see the glory of the Lord, the majesty of our God. Strengthen the weak hands, and make firm the feeble knees. Say to those who are of a fearful heart, 'Be strong, do not fear! Here is your God. He will come with vengeance, with terrible recompense. He will come and save you.' Then the eyes of the blind shall be opened, and the ears of the deaf unstopped; then the lame shall leap like a deer, and the tongue of the speechless sing for joy. For waters shall break forth in the wilderness, and streams in the desert... A highway shall be there, and it shall be called the Holy Way; the unclean shall not travel on it, but it shall be for God's people... And the ransomed of the Lord shall return, and come to Zion with singing; everlasting joy shall be upon their heads; they shall obtain joy and gladness, and sorrow and sighing shall flee away.

Here is the vision of God's rule: the wilderness blossoming, people cured of their disabilities, the ravenous beasts fled away and with them all sorrow and sighing. It is part of the Advent story because of the way it tells of God's coming rule. It gives us something to hope for and look forward to, in the sense of knowing that everything one day will be all right. As Julian of Norwich assured us in the 14th century, 'All shall be well, and all manner of thing shall be well.'

Despite the flipside of this idea, as we saw two days ago – the idea that we might be fooled into laziness of thought and action in this world because we're pinning our hopes on the next – we need this vision. 'Where there is no vision, the people perish' (Proverbs 29:18, KJV). It has a sustaining quality that can carry us through all sorts of agony and the long dull ache of keeping going.

For me, it's never the sharp, dramatic experience that is so difficult, as adrenalin gets me through that, almost before I have worked out what is happening. It's the time later, after the disorientating pain has subsided, that seems so hard, when I've just got to keep on keeping on. After I was diagnosed with cancer, I was warned that one of the worst times for most patients is when the treatment is over. After you've finished the various treatments (surgery, chemotherapy, radiotherapy and the various side-effects and reactions that they bring), everyone else expects you to be happier and perhaps feeling a sense of relief. Actually, though, you feel a kind of loss. In a selfish sense, you're no longer the centre of attention, the patient whom your family, friends and the medical staff need to help and be kind to. In a more creditable way, you miss the routine of the hospital and the reassuring presence of the nurses and doctors. You're no longer carried along by the tide of the crisis and the need to gear yourself up for the next round of treatment – although you might well still be feeling exhausted and ill – so it's a letdown. In addition, you're faced with a huge, looming uncertainty: no one can be 100 per cent sure whether the treatment has worked. Have you still got cancer or not?

Even years later, if the treatment seems to have been successful, the experience is like what Alan Bennett describes in *Untold Stories* (Faber, 2005), when the doctor tells him that all is well, five years after his initial treatment for bowel cancer:

> The habit (and the precaution) of treating whatever happens as provisional is hard to lose. So, though I'm cheerful, I don't rejoice or dare to think I'm cured – though in statistical terms, five years without a recurrence would qualify. Actually I daren't think that lest

I activate the laws of irony and the opposite
happens.

When you've finished the medical interventions, nobody
can tell for sure, so you just have to carry on and resume
normal life. But life will never be the same again: everything has shifted, and you're no longer the same person.
It's similar to the time, just a little while after a funeral,
when others think that you must already have got over
your bereavement. Some people think you should have
pulled yourself together by now, when actually the drawn-
out agony of loss is only just beginning.

This is just when you need the vision offered by Isaiah. It
is exactly what Tennyson found after the death of Arthur
Hallam. He imagined Arthur's being in heaven, while he
was left behind in this world with his memories:

> But I remained, whose hopes were dim,
>   Whose life, whose thoughts were little worth,
>   To wander on a darkened earth,
> Where all things round me breathed of him.

From this low state, he still sensed his friend's positive
influence and eventually found some kind of strength:

I felt and feel, though left alone,
His being working in mine own,
The footsteps of his life in mine…

And so my passion hath not swerved
To works of weakness, but I find
An image comforting the mind,
And in my grief a strength reserved.

From *In Memoriam*

For reflection

Can you think of someone who has influenced you and helped you towards a more positive vision? Can you reflect on what they gave you that sustained you through dark times? Thank God for them.

11 December

Isaiah 40:1–4a, 6–8, 10–11 (KJV, abridged)

Strength and lovingkindness together

Comfort ye, comfort ye my people, saith your God. Speak ye comfortably to Jerusalem, and cry unto her, that her warfare is accomplished, that her iniquity is pardoned: for she hath received of the Lord's hand double for all her sins. The voice of him that crieth in the wilderness, Prepare ye the way of the Lord, make straight in the desert a highway for our God. Every valley shall be exalted, and every mountain and hill shall be made low... The voice said, Cry. And he said, What shall I cry? All flesh is grass, and all the goodliness thereof is as the flower of the field: The grass withereth, the flower fadeth: because the spirit of the Lord bloweth upon it: surely the people is grass. The grass withereth, the flower fadeth: but the word of our God shall stand forever... Behold, the Lord God will come with strong hand... He shall feed his flock like a shepherd: he shall gather the lambs with his arm, and carry them in his bosom, and shall gently lead those that are with young.

Like much great poetry, this passage from Isaiah offers a telling combination of something warmly familiar along with the thrill of recognising a truth. We have heard these words so many times over the years, perhaps in dark and cold churches at this time of year, when we might sense that the words have not changed, while we ourselves have altered; but their reassuring message of God's comfort also gives us the satisfying sense of recognising the ways in which God meets our needs. We can relate it to our own experience.

All this is in a rich mix with a further challenging element, for Isaiah's message isn't just a little boost when we're a bit tired because we've overdone things. No, it is wondrous balm to the broken soul, deep peace after many struggles. We can experience that peace much more deeply after we have suffered. And, of course, we know that no one escapes suffering in this world. In verse 2, where the KJV says, 'that her warfare is accomplished', the NRSV translates, 'that she has served her term, that her penalty is paid'. We have paid our debts now.

After recalling for us the Lord's highway, which we heard about yesterday from Isaiah 35, chapter 40 is the setting for one of the Bible's great reminders of our mortality: 'All flesh is grass... The grass withereth, the flower fadeth:

but the word of our God shall stand forever' (vv. 6–8). Again, this chimes with our experience of our ageing, fading bodies – for most of us, anyway, over a certain age. We might feel feeble and increasingly frail, but God is like a solid rock. This is the good news, and it comes in just the way we need it. For the Lord will come both in power and might (v. 10) and in gentleness, tenderly gathering us into his arms (v. 11).

Depending on our personality, we might prefer to emphasise one aspect rather than the other, either appreciating the strength and triumph of our king or finding comfort in the lovingkindness of the shepherd of our souls. But the fact is that the two qualities are woven inextricably together. God is in both.

These are vital Advent themes – the coming of the Lord who is both a mighty conquering hero and a tender loving comforter. Tennyson takes us further into this stirring combination at the beginning of *In Memoriam*, when he brings together the 'Strong Son of God' with the gentle creator to whom he can appeal for forgiveness for being so obsessed with his grief. He describes his fragile faith (perhaps as feeble as our bodies) and prays for it to grow stronger:

Strong Son of God, immortal Love,
*   Whom we, that have not seen thy face,*
*   By faith, and faith alone, embrace,*
Believing where we cannot prove…

We have but faith: we cannot know;
*   For knowledge is of things we see;*
*   And yet we trust it comes from thee,*
A beam in darkness: let it grow.

Let knowledge grow from more to more,
*   But more of reverence in us dwell;*
*   That mind and soul, according well,*
May make one music as before,

But vaster…

Forgive my grief for one removed,
*   Thy creature, whom I found so fair.*
*   I trust he lives in thee, and there*
I find him worthier to be loved.

There are times when it seems that this is all we can manage to do – to pray that we might hold fast to God through the storms and pain that will come our way. We can at least remember that God is merciful and thank him for all of his creatures. So, with Tennyson, we can ask for forgiveness and wisdom:

Forgive these wild and wandering cries,
  Confusions of a wasted youth;
    Forgive them where they fail in truth,
And in thy wisdom make me wise.

From Prologue, *In Memoriam*

For reflection

Are there any matters lying on your conscience about which you doubt God's forgiveness, where you think you might have wandered off from his ways? If so, could you begin to pray about them?

12 December

Isaiah 40:26–31 (KJV)

Revival after the storm

Lift up your eyes on high, and behold who hath created these things, that bringeth out their host by number: he calleth them all by names by the greatness of his might, for that he is strong in power; not one faileth. Why sayest thou, O Jacob, and speakest, O Israel, My way is hid from the Lord, and my judgment is passed over from my God? Hast thou not known? hast thou not heard, that the everlasting God, the Lord, the Creator of the ends of the earth, fainteth not, neither is weary? there is no searching of his understanding. He giveth power to the faint; and to them that have no might he increaseth strength. Even the youths shall faint and be weary, and the young men shall utterly fall: But they that wait upon the Lord shall renew their strength; they shall mount up with wings as eagles; they shall run, and not be weary; and they shall walk, and not faint.

Following on from yesterday's passage, these verses bring together the themes of God's comfort and strength. In the Oscar-winning film *Chariots of Fire* (1981), about the athlete Eric Liddell, it is this passage that Eric reads out when he preaches in church on a Sunday – the very day when he should have been running in the Olympics. Having refused to take part on the Lord's day, instead he stands in the pulpit and tells of God's power, before going on to win a different Olympic race, run on a different day.

The film emphasises the contrast between bodily strength, despite which even youthful Olympic athletes will 'faint and be weary', and the inner strength that comes from the Lord. As we saw yesterday, we all know about feeling weary, perhaps through illness or lack of sleep, after childbirth or from sheer old age. I remember the way the feeling suddenly hit me after I had been in hospital: it seemed like a wall rising up out of nowhere to knock me down, and I could barely move.

But, after all this wringing out, when we've gone through the barrier of paralysis by exhaustion, usually there comes a time when we're surprised by feeling just a little better. Perhaps we're not much better or we feel it only for a few moments, but we sense a return of some faculties: some power is still in us and we wake refreshed. This is when we can feel that the Lord renews our strength (v. 31).

In the middle of those moments when the tiredness squeezes out everything else, if I can manage to put two thoughts together, sometimes I think of a line of Anglo-Saxon poetry from '*Deor*', a tenth-century lament for better times. Its refrain goes, '*Thaes ofereode; thisses swa maeg*', which translates as something like, 'That passed away; so may this pass from me.' It reminds me of the fact that good and bad times both come and go; the dawn will come, even after what seems like the darkest, most interminable night.

Henry Vaughan's poem 'The Revival' speaks of this – the startling joy that can arrive, seemingly out of nowhere, perhaps after we have given up hope. The poem suggests stirrings of new life after 'night, frost and storms', which could be experiences such as bereavement or the loss of things we hold dear, such as jobs, homes and relationships.

> *Unfold, unfold! Take in His light,*
> *Who makes thy cares more short than night.*
> *The joys, which with His day-star rise,*
> *He deals to all but drowsy eyes;*
> *And, what the men of this world miss,*
> *Some drops and dews of future bliss.*
>   *Hark! how His winds have chang'd their note!*
> *And with warm whispers call thee out;*
> *The frosts are past, the storms are gone,*
> *And backward life at last comes on.*

The lofty groves in express joys
Reply unto the turtle's voice,
And here in dust and dirt, O here
The lilies of His love appear!

Unlikely as it seems, things really can get better. When we had given up hope that our situation could change, suddenly 'life at last comes on'. We had buried everything so deeply underground, but the Lord is beyond all our imaginings. He has wondrous plans for us to stay with him.

For reflection

A similar idea is expressed in a more well-known poem by George Herbert (1593–1633), 'The Flower':

How fresh, O Lord, how sweet and clean
Are thy returns! ev'n as the flowers in spring…
Grief melts away
Like snow in May,
As if there were no such cold thing…
Who would have thought my shrivelled heart
Could have recovered greenness? It was gone
Quite underground…

These are thy wonders, Lord of love,
To make us see we are but flowers that glide;
Which when we once can find and prove,
Thou hast a garden for us, where to bide.

13 December (Samuel Johnson)

Matthew 13:44–46, 51–52 (KJV)

Unshowy but deep faith

Again, the kingdom of heaven is like unto treasure hid in a field; the which when a man hath found, he hideth, and for joy thereof goeth and selleth all that he hath, and buyeth that field. Again, the kingdom of heaven is like unto a merchant man, seeking goodly pearls: Who, when he had found one pearl of great price, went and sold all that he had, and bought it... Jesus saith unto them, Have ye understood all these things? They say unto him, Yea, Lord. Then said he unto them, Therefore every scribe which is instructed unto the kingdom of heaven is like unto a man that is an householder, which bringeth forth out of his treasure things new and old.

It is fitting that this is the day when the Anglican Church commemorates the writer and dictionary compiler Samuel Johnson (1709–84), who died on 13 December. He was a firm supporter of the Church of England and was celebrated in his lifetime for his strong faith: people called him the 'Great Moralist', 'then a term of affection and honour', as it says in *Exciting Holiness: Collects and readings for festivals and lesser festivals of the calendar* (ed. Brother Tristam SSF, Canterbury Press, 2003). That book sets out readings (including the one above) to mark this day, designating Johnson as being among 'Men and women of learning'.

Having been haunted – terrified, even – by the fear of death for much of his life, Johnson might have relished the appropriateness of dying in Advent, the church's season for thinking about death and judgement. Much of his writing focused on themes of this season, such as penitence. There is the famous story of his own act of penance in the marketplace in Uttoxeter, not far from Lichfield, the city where he grew up. As a young man, Johnson had refused one day to work on the bookstall that his father ran. Years later, in his 60s and long after his father's death but now ashamed of his disobedient behaviour, he returned to Uttoxeter and stood alone in the market square in the rain, bare-headed, for several hours.

Johnson knew from the inside that God's kingdom is like the pearl of great price: it is the one still centre around which all else moves, and the only thing that really matters. Some people might think his penance in the marketplace was pointless, but his conscience knew better. He needed to express his sorrow and his turning away from selfishness in a tangible way.

In his biography of the writer, John Wain notes that Johnson's religion was not one of 'blazing vision and hosanna'. Johnson's dictionary defines 'pious' as 'Careful of the duties owed by created beings to God.' All this sounds deeply unfashionable: 'moralist', 'pious' and 'duties' are hardly buzz words in current evangelism (or the rest of life). Very English in his reserve, Johnson was genuinely and profoundly Christian. It is not just those who cry 'Lord, Lord' who will enter the kingdom of heaven. Perhaps he is the patron saint of unshowy but deep faith.

The prayer below is one that Johnson wrote for New Year, so it's appropriate now, soon after the church's new year at Advent and just before the secular one on 1 January. He committed himself to special self-examination on particular days in the year, including New Year's Day, Good Friday, the anniversary of his beloved wife's death and his own birthday. He composed this prayer so that he could memorise it and use it throughout the year. It begins by setting human life within God's reign ('by whose mercy my life has been yet prolonged…') and echoes Advent themes, most obviously death ('when thou shalt call me hence…'). As in his definition of 'pious', he conveys a strong sense of being under the creator's loving gaze, despite the distractions of the cares of the world. Sometimes it is a struggle to keep our attention on the pearl of great price.

Johnson is also refreshingly unsentimental about growing older: not for him the easy golden glow of thoughts about the wisdom of age. He knows its 'evils', which threaten to overwhelm us all. So this is a fitting prayer for Advent, when we can try to see ourselves against the background of heaven and ask our Father to increase our awareness of his lovingkindness towards us.

Prayer by Dr Johnson

Almighty God, by whose mercy my life has been yet
*   prolonged to another year,*
grant that thy mercy may not be vain.
Let not my years be multiplied to increase my guilt,
but as age advances, let me become
more pure in my thoughts,
more regular in my desires, and
more obedient to thy laws.
Let not the cares of the world distract me,
nor the evils of age overwhelm me.
But continue and increase thy lovingkindness
*   towards me,*
and when thou shalt call me hence,
receive me to everlasting happiness,
for the sake of Jesus Christ, our Lord. Amen

14 December (St John of the Cross)

1 Corinthians 2:3–5, 7, 9–10 (KJV)

The mysteries
of the dark night

And I was with you in weakness, and in fear, and in much trembling. And my speech and my preaching was not with enticing words of man's wisdom, but in demonstration of the Spirit and of power: That your faith should not stand in the wisdom of men, but in the power of God... But we speak the wisdom of God in a mystery, even the hidden wisdom, which God ordained before the world unto our glory... But as it is written, Eye hath not seen, nor ear heard, neither have entered into the heart of man, the things which God hath prepared for them that love him. But God hath revealed them unto us by his Spirit: for the Spirit searcheth all things, yea, the deep things of God.

Today is the commemoration of St John of the Cross, a Spanish monk who died on this day in 1591. We might wonder what he has to say to us, having lived such a distant and different life from ours, but his poetry and mystical writings describe an experience that is a vital part of the life of faith – the dark night of the soul. This is a time of testing, in which helpful props, such as warm emotions or a sense of God's presence, seem to have melted away and you feel very much on your own. Such a state – dry, dark and apparently hopeless – can last for years, and can demand the utmost commitment from the Christian. Prayer comes to seem pointless; worship leaves you cold. It is a time of purification, in which you just have to cling on to faith, however bleak it seems. If you can get through this, you can cope with almost anything else that might be thrown at you.

T.S. Eliot, in *Burnt Norton*, describes the value that this long wait can have: darkness can 'purify the soul', which has a distinct Advent feel to it. It can prepare you for more depth, clearing out your accumulated emotional, physical and spiritual baggage and leaving you in a state of readiness. John of the Cross writes about this experience, with a sense of waiting with God, turning to him in the darkness and uncertainty, while being purified by God's fire:

Though in pitch-darkness, with no ray,
Entirely I am burned away...

The more benightedly it darkens,
Turns more to that to which it hearkens,
Though in pitch-darkness, with no ray.
From 'With a Divine Intention' (trans. Roy Campbell)

So, if we keep on turning to him, even in the darkness, God purges away the bad in us. Even when nothing seems to be happening – we feel absolutely nothing – it's up to us to carry on seeking him regardless, in prayer, Bible study, worship, spiritual reading, service, our dealings with others and so on.

The poem continues by developing John's thinking about the value of this time of purification: it can draw us nearer to God. Ultimately, God will work within us:

Since I knew Love, I have been taught
He can perform most wondrous labours.
Though good and bad in me are neighbours
He turns their difference to naught...

John of the Cross had a rough life himself, having been brought up by a widowed mother, educated at a charity school and even thrown into prison for his work with his monastic order. Yet it was his experience in prison that enabled him to produce his most powerful writing. Like many others before him and since, he drew on his suffering, so that good could come out of ill. He sought out the positive aspects of it, in the sense of Psalm 84:6: 'Who going through the vale of misery use it for a well' (Book of Common Prayer).

Today's passage from 1 Corinthians appears to have been chosen for the commemoration of John of the Cross because he was a small man, as well as being from a humble background. He wasn't superficially impressive. Yet he achieved a great deal, and his writings are still cherished for the way in which they unlock something vital about our relationship with God. We've all had some experience of approaching other people 'in weakness, and in fear, and in much trembling' (v. 3), and lacking 'enticing words of man's wisdom' (v. 4).

It was surely a shared sense of this weakness that made the 2010 film *The King's Speech* a worldwide hit and an Oscar winner, as it told of King George VI's struggle to come to terms with his stammer. Those who are old enough to remember the king's broadcasts in the 1930s and '40s refer to the bonding experience of willing him on – praying that he would get to the end of the speech without breaking down. Even though he was a king and emperor, there was a strong human fellow-feeling that everyone could respond to.

What Paul is looking at, though, incorporates this feeling and takes it further. It is something more than just a lack of fluency: he is talking about the way that God's wisdom is different from the world's. It is hidden: 'even the hidden wisdom, which God ordained before the world unto our glory'. We will always struggle to understand it in this life. This is one of 'the deep things of God'. So, in the dark night of the soul, God seems to take away his own gifts of comfort and the sense of his presence. It doesn't make human sense; it is only by God's Spirit that we can approach these mysteries (v. 10).

For reflection

O God, the judge of all, who gave your servant John of the Cross a warmth of nature, a strength of purpose and a mystical faith that sustained him even in the darkness: shed your light on all who love you and grant them union of body and soul in your Son Jesus Christ our Lord. Amen

Collect for the Commemoration of St John of the Cross

❧ Week 3 ❧

Tracking God's Wisdom

Here, in the third week of Advent, we move ahead with the story as the old order gives way to the new. So we read of Elisha taking over from Elijah; John the Baptist preaching repentance – in a central part of Advent teaching – and then the strands of Jesus' lineage, John's parents, and Joseph and Mary. As we move ever nearer to Christmas, we also get ready to meet our Lord by thinking over various aspects of God, using the Advent antiphons, which focus on a range of different titles for him and thus emphasise the richness of his love.

The poems that take us through this week range from medieval prayers to biting observations by George Herbert, to the mournful farewells of Tennyson. As ever, they take us more deeply into various Bible stories and also, crucially, into their implications for us now. So, for example, W.H. Auden's retelling of the Christmas story in his 'Christmas Oratorio', *For the Time Being*, draws out Joseph's questions, which in many cases match our own.

Despite being a deeply religious man, Auden doesn't seem to be quoted as often as he deserves in Christian circles. He wasn't outwardly respectable like T.S. Eliot, and the taint lingered long of his flight to America in the late 1930s, which was seen as an attempt to duck out of the war. In many ways, his poems are easier to understand than those of Eliot; they often make sense immediately, but yield more on later readings. *For the Time Being* is an amazing reimagining of the Christmas story in modern terms. It was dedicated to his mother, a devout Christian, as it was written soon after her death; her influence remained with Auden strongly all his life.

15 December

2 Kings 2:9–12 (NRSV)

'Bound by gold chains about the feet of God'

Elijah said to Elisha, 'Tell me what I may do for you, before I am taken from you.' Elisha said, 'Please let me inherit a double share of your spirit.' He responded, 'You have asked a hard thing; yet, if you see me as I am being taken from you, it will be granted you; if not, it will not.' As they continued walking and talking, a chariot of fire and horses of fire separated the two of them, and Elijah ascended in a whirlwind into heaven. Elisha kept watching and crying out, 'Father, father! The chariots of Israel and its horsemen!' But when he could no longer see him, he grasped his own clothes and tore them in two pieces.

After the Advent themes of penance and purgation, seen in the writings of both Samuel Johnson and John of the Cross, today's reading takes us back to another part of the story – the prophets and the new age dawning. As Elisha takes over from Elijah, we have that sense again of patient waiting on the Lord. It emphasises our dependence on his mercy and our absolute need for him, despite the realisation that his holiness is beyond our comprehension and so far above our own sinfulness.

As usual, there are healthy and unhealthy ways to look at this. We can wallow in our wickedness, bowed down by our imperfections and the knowledge that we will never be good enough, or we can be drawn up to strive for goodness, strengthened by God's love for us.

We will never be perfect, but God loves us even in our imperfections. This must be hard to understand for people who have never known secure, unwavering love from parents and then from friends and a partner. Human affection and loyalty from those around us may be only a pale reflection of God's care for us, but it is a gift from him by which we can approach the wonders of his perfect love. It is a grounding in our true purpose in life: to spread the love of God. Knowing that we are rooted and enfolded in God's care, we can grow to share this care with others.

One of the times when this can feel like a tall order is when we feel inadequate for the tasks before us, especially in comparison with our mentors and earlier generations. That is the focus of today's passage about Elisha. Elisha wanted desperately to be like Elijah, and his request for a double share of his spirit is a touching sign of his neediness and lack of confidence. Those of us who have never lived through a world war might sometimes have a similar sense: we've never been called up to fight or struggled through deprivation, hard grind and debilitating fear on the home front. As one character says at the end of *King Lear*, 'The oldest hath borne most: we that are young / Shall never see so much, nor live so long.'

Tennyson famously dramatises this feeling in '*Morte d'Arthur*', which was written soon after his best friend's death in 1833 (and published in 1842). Beneath its mythological setting about the death of King Arthur, it is about the end of one age and the dawning of a new one – but, crucially, also about the necessity of letting go. We can't cling on to all the things of the past, however comforting it may be and however wonderful they were. We can't just pretend that the situation has not moved on, leaving us behind. Our friends have gone, those we loved have died, and we feel that we are alone. As Sir Bedivere says in the poem:

> *For now I see the true old times are dead,*
> *When every morning brought a noble chance,*
> *And every chance brought out a noble knight…*
> *And I, the last, go forth companionless,*
> *And the days darken round me, and the years,*
> *Among new men, strange faces, other minds.*

Arthur replies in a justly celebrated passage, which I've heard read at funerals (though I don't know how anyone could stay dry-eyed while hearing it):

> *The old order changeth, yielding place to new,*
> *And God fulfils himself in many ways,*
> *Lest one good custom should corrupt the world.*

This response is absolutely right for Advent, which is, after all, the church's New Year. There ought to be more of a sense of clearing away the old in preparation for the new. Our personal baggage and other debris have cluttered our life, and now we need to clean it away and focus on what is truly important. As Arthur, facing death, continues:

> *Pray for my soul. More things are wrought by prayer*
> *Than this world dreams of. Wherefore, let thy voice*
> *Rise like a fountain for me night and day.*
> *For what are men better than sheep or goats*
> *That nourish a blind life within the brain,*
> *If, knowing God, they lift not hands of prayer*
> *Both for themselves and those who call them friend?*
> *For so the whole round earth is every way*
> *Bound by gold chains about the feet of God.*

Here we are granted a vision of the whole created order under God's rule. Our purpose is not to carve out some version of success for ourselves: that would be an illusion, especially in a world where so many things are beyond us and our control. Rather, here we get a glimpse of our place under God. We pray to him because we can't do anything else. We are compelled by love to turn to him – not in a bad sense of being forced but in a healthy sense of carrying out what we were created by him to do. He made us in love, and we return that love to him and reflect it to others.

For reflection

Thank God for the people who have influenced you in the past in your faith, and try thinking of one or two ways in which you could draw on their spirit (in Elisha's sense) in the next few days of Advent.

102

16 December

Luke 3:7–8, 10–11, 15–16 (NRSV, abridged)

'Ye, whose hopes rely on God… repent'

John said to the crowds that came out to be baptised by him, 'You brood of vipers! Who warned you to flee from the wrath to come? Bear fruits worthy of repentance…' And the crowds asked him, 'What then should we do?' In reply he said to them, 'Whoever has two coats must share with anyone who has none; and whoever has food must do likewise.' … As the people were filled with expectation, and all were questioning in their hearts concerning John, whether he might be the Messiah, John answered all of them by saying, 'I baptise you with water; but one who is more powerful than I is coming; I am not worthy to untie the thong of his sandals. He will baptise you with the Holy Spirit and fire.'

John the Baptist is one of the main figures of Advent, and traditionally the church remembers him on the third Sunday of the season, which usually falls at about this point in December. So here he is, in many ways the last of the Old Testament prophets, preaching repentance of sins. He draws the crowds to follow him out to the desert, not because of a comfortable message but by a rare combination of visible integrity and tough truth-telling. They can see that he practises what he preaches, living in the wilderness and rejecting material security. They also recognise, if only dimly, that what he says is right. They know, deep down, that they are sinners and need to repent.

So they ask, 'What then should we do?' (v. 10). John's reply is perhaps surprising in that he doesn't focus on personal salvation or individual soul-searching – as we might if we were to address those questions today (influenced as we are by a culture of popular psychology and self-help books). Instead, he concentrates on simple actions that anyone can take, such as sharing resources with those who are less well-off ('Whoever has two coats…').

These are outward gestures, though, which don't necess-arily imply deep inner convictions. Perhaps John is try-ing to get away from empty words and easy promises, or perhaps he is suggesting that when we start doing the right thing, we might also begin to think the right thing. The second of these possibilities reflects the way in which we can sometimes surprise ourselves when we try out something new: perhaps being generous wasn't as difficult as we had feared or we realise suddenly how immensely rewarding it is to help others.

As C.S. Lewis says in *Mere Christianity* (1952):

> Do not waste time bothering whether you 'love' your neighbour. Act as if you did. When you behave as if you loved someone, you will presently come to love him. If you injure someone you dislike you will find yourself disliking him more. If you do him a good turn you will find yourself disliking him less.

John the Baptist is such a compelling, extremist figure that we wouldn't normally associate him with such a suck-it-and-see approach, but he might also be suggesting that we have to start somewhere. Most of us now find it easier to associate his call to repentance with what we think of as really big sins – perhaps adultery or a life of crime – when actually we need to apply his message to our everyday decisions, the way we treat others and whether we go the extra mile to help out. We can't afford to let his message die on the wind, as one poet so vividly imagines as he conjures up an image of John in the desert:

Parched body, hollow eyes, some uncouth thing
Made him appear, long since from Earth exiled.

There burst he forth; All ye, whose hopes rely
On God, with me amidst these deserts mourn,
Repent, repent, and from old errors turn!
Who listened to his voice, obeyed his cry?

Only the echoes which he made relent,
Rung from their marble caves, Repent, repent.
From 'For the Baptist'

This poem was written by William Drummond of Hawthornden (1585–1649). The fact that its message from 400 years ago seems as necessary as ever today only reinforces the continuing need for it – in John the Baptist's original hearers, Drummond's 17th-century audience and the people of our own time. Our recalcitrant human nature is always reluctant to change. We need to pray hard to break the cycle in our own hearts. Can you think of at least one thing that you could do this week to change your familiar patterns, which could help others?

For prayer

Almighty God, by whose providence your servant John the Baptist was wonderfully born, and sent to prepare the way of your Son our Saviour by the preaching of repentance: lead us to repent according to his preaching and, after his example, constantly to speak the truth, boldly to rebuke vice, and patiently to suffer for the truth's sake; through Jesus Christ your Son our Lord, who is alive and reigns with you, in the unity of the Holy Spirit, one God, now and forever. Amen

Collect for the Festival of the Birth of John the Baptist, Common Worship

17 December (O Sapientia)

Matthew 1:1–2, 5–7, 16–17 (KJV, abridged)

Tracing God's Wisdom through our lives

The book of the generation of Jesus Christ, the son of David, the son of Abraham. Abraham begat Isaac; and Isaac begat Jacob; and Jacob begat Judas and his brethren... and Booz begat Obed of Ruth; and Obed begat Jesse; And Jesse begat David the king; and David the king begat Solomon of her that had been the wife of Urias; And Solomon begat Roboam... And Jacob begat Joseph the husband of Mary, of whom was born Jesus, who is called Christ. So all the generations from Abraham to David are fourteen generations; and from David until the carrying away into Babylon are fourteen generations; and from the carrying away into Babylon unto Christ are fourteen generations.

This is just the sort of passage that many Bible-reading plans or lectionaries miss out. But I think there is something quietly wonderful, moving and poetic about this catalogue of exotic names – especially if you try to read them out loud. Even when I stumble over the names, they conjure up distant, exotic lands and people. They are similar to the wonderful array of peoples who heard the disciples at Pentecost (Acts 2:9–11).

The playwright Christopher Marlowe (1564–93) achieves a similar effect in *Tamburlaine the Great* (1590), which tells of the rise of the all-conquering King Tamburlaine as he sweeps across the world, subduing everyone in his path:

> *Is it not passing brave to be a king,*
> *And ride in triumph through Persepolis?…*
> *Kings of Argier, Morocco, and of Fez,*
> *You that have march'd with happy Tamburlaine*
> *As far as from the frozen plage of heaven*
> *Unto the watery Morning's ruddy bower,*
> *And thence by land unto the torrid zone…*

The naming of places and people conveys tremendous power, as is suggested in many traditional stories, including those in the Old Testament where God reveals his mysterious name, 'I am', and thus something of his nature (Exodus 3:14).

The genealogy is there in Matthew's opening words to emphasise Jesus' place in the history of Israel. It was important to the gospel writers to show that God was working throughout history and to trace Jesus back to King David, so that Jesus was seen as the culmination of all these generations. The complete list also mentions four women, which wasn't usual in this type of family tree. All of them – Tamar, Rahab, Ruth and the wife of Urias (Uriah) – were Gentiles, which could suggest something about God's inclusiveness. God can draw in even those who are outside the chosen people.

The recital of Jesus' family line can also remind us that God's plans have a particular logic to them. God has been working all along, through the history of these generations. For us, the point may be that things don't usually feel as neat as this, even though God is with us throughout it all. So often, our own lives don't seem to have any such pattern. Someone who writes very vividly about this observation is Sister Maria Boulding, a Benedictine nun who died in 2009 at the age of 80. She was a great spiritual writer whose book about Advent, *The Coming of God* (originally published in 1982, and now available from Canterbury Press), is simply the best thing I've ever read about the season. (And while we're on family trees, I'm also delighted that she turns out to be a distant cousin of mine: we have a great-great-great-grandfather in common.)

Sister Maria writes about her own life as 'a tapestry, from the wrong side' (*A Touch of God*, SPCK, 1982). When looking at her own vocation, she takes the familiar idea of life's rich tapestry a stage further. She traces the threads of God's calling to her over a number of years. Most of the time, random events seemed like an odd collection of knots and twists – just like the back of a tapestry. But she realises that these odd lines do form some sort of pattern, and even a beautiful shape. She can't recognise much of it now, but she knows that God can see it and that she will find out about it eventually (and I guess that is what she is doing at the moment, in heaven).

This sense of God's planning in the generations leading up to Jesus leads on to the title that is traditionally given by the church to this day, 17 December: 'O Sapientia' ('O Wisdom'). On this day, some churches read or sing the first of the Advent antiphons, the 'Great O Antiphons'. These are a collection of seven short prayers, originally in Latin, used on each of the days from 17 to 23 December (although there is some variety to the traditions: the Book of Common Prayer starts them on 16 December). They focus on seven titles of Jesus, reflecting the various different biblical promises and prophecies that he fulfils: O Wisdom, O Adonai, O Root of Jesse, O Key of David, O Dayspring, O King of the Nations and O Emmanuel.

The point is that these titles show what Jesus can become for all of us: he can grow within us to be our Dayspring, King and so on. Each of the short prayers of the Antiphons builds up to the word 'Come', and ends by asking God, 'Come and teach us, save us, bring us light.' Some churches use them in a service by reading them out or singing them, followed by a verse of the hymn 'O come, O come, Emmanuel', which is itself based on the antiphons.

The sequence starts today with Wisdom, God's Wisdom, in the line traced through Old Testament books such as Proverbs and Ecclesiastes. In these books, Wisdom is portrayed as a female figure, whom the writers recommend seeking out. We need to search for God's wise plans for humankind, just as Matthew did in tracing Jesus' family line.

For reflection

It is part of the Christian spiritual tradition that God dwells in the centre of every man, an unseen, largely unknown Strength and Wisdom, moving him to be human, to grow and to expand his humanity to the utmost of its capacity.

Christopher Bryant (1905–85)

18 December (O Adonai)

Matthew 1:18–21 (KJV)

Questions at the heart
of the story

Now the birth of Jesus Christ was on this wise: When as his mother Mary was espoused to Joseph, before they came together, she was found with child of the Holy Ghost. Then Joseph her husband, being a just man, and not willing to make her a publick example, was minded to put her away privily. But while he thought on these things, behold, the angel of the Lord appeared unto him in a dream, saying, Joseph, thou son of David, fear not to take unto thee Mary thy wife: for that which is conceived in her is of the Holy Ghost. And she shall bring forth a son, and thou shalt call his name JESUS: for he shall save his people from their sins.

This passage takes us into really familiar territory. If we can make an effort to listen afresh – as if we haven't heard it read at many, many carol services – we might find something that speaks to our experience with a different type of familiarity. Many of its themes follow on from yesterday's passage from the same chapter in Matthew's gospel, in that it continues with the sense that God's plans may seem odd and difficult to us. Who would have guessed (certainly not Joseph) that any good could come out of something so shameful and seemingly wicked as a baby's arrival out of wedlock, especially in such a traditional community? God's ways are very strange. Joseph could have been forgiven for wondering why on earth God seemed to be deliberately using the most bizarre means to unfold his purposes.

Today's Advent antiphon may give us a clue: 'O Adonai' is the title of God for 18 December. It means 'Masters' or 'My Lords' in the plural, and might suggest God's rule rising above all our petty ideas of what he should be doing. So often, it can be hard to follow God's paths, when both our worldly wisdom and our desire for our own comfort can pull us in another direction. George Herbert captures this feeling vividly in a poem that has become a favourite with many: 'The Collar'. It probes our sense of self-righteousness when the life of faith seems grim and we're feeling sorry for ourselves, as the writer imagines his inner voice tempting him to be free of what seem like the constraints and sorrows of religion.

I struck the board, and cry'd, No more.
        I will abroad.
    What? shall I ever sigh and pine?
My lines and life are free; free as the road,
    Loose as the wind, as large as store.
        Shall I be still in suit?
    Have I no harvest but a thorn
    To let me blood, and not restore
    What I have lost with cordial fruit?
        Sure there was wine
Before my sighs did dry it: there was corn
        Before my tears did drown it...
    Not so, my heart: but there is fruit,
        And thou hast hands.
    Recover all thy sigh-blown age
On double pleasures; leave thy cold dispute
Of what is fit, and not. Forsake thy cage...
        He that forbears
        To suit and serve his need,
        Deserves his load.
But as I rav'd, and grew more fierce and wild
        At every word,
    Me thoughts I heard one calling, Child!
        And I reply'd, My Lord.

Sometimes, being a decent Christian seems to be so much effort and to involve boring duties, interminable meetings, mind-numbing arguments and prickly people. It can all feel like a waste of time and energy, sapping what strength we have. Other people seem to manage well enough without it, too... But we know, we know: it's the truth, and it has laid itself on our heart. We were made for God and, as Augustine said, our heart will be restless until it rests in him.

We can try to follow God's mysterious ways, to stay close in his love through the tortuous windings of our pilgrimage in this world, as Joseph had to do. W.H. Auden dramatises part of this experience in *For the Time Being*, his long series of poems about the nativity story. In the section 'The Temptation of St Joseph', he imagines Joseph tormented by taunting:

> *Mary may be pure,*
> *But, Joseph, are you sure?*
> *How is one to tell?*
> *Suppose, for instance... Well...*

Not surprisingly, Joseph asks the angel Gabriel to tell him the reason behind these strange events. When the reply is a firm 'No', he continues, in an attempt to fathom Mary's actions:

All I ask is one
Important and elegant proof
That what my Love had done
Was really at your will
And that your will is Love.

Gabriel responds:

No, you must believe;
Be silent, and sit still.

A narrator then fills in some of the gaps, urging Joseph:

Forgetting nothing and believing all,
You must behave as if this were not strange at all...

To choose what is difficult all one's days
As if it were easy, that is faith.

Joseph's bewilderment here seems all too familiar. He sheds light on our own wonderings and doubts, when our life seems like a tapestry seen from the wrong side. So our modern questions are there at the heart of the Christmas story.

For prayer

*God our Father, who from the family of your
servant David raised up Joseph the carpenter
to be the guardian of your incarnate Son and
husband of the Blessed Virgin Mary: give us
grace to follow him in faithful obedience to your
commands; through Jesus Christ your Son our
Lord. Amen*

Collect for the Festival of St Joseph of Nazareth (19 March),
Common Worship

19 December (O Root of Jesse)

Luke 1:6–7, 11–13, 18–20 (KJV)

Claiming the tradition as our own

And [Zacharias and Elisabeth] were both righteous before God, walking in all the commandments and ordinances of the Lord blameless. And they had no child... And there appeared unto him an angel of the Lord standing on the right side of the altar of incense. And when Zacharias saw him, he was troubled, and fear fell upon him. But the angel said unto him, Fear not, Zacharias: for thy prayer is heard; and thy wife Elisabeth shall bear thee a son, and thou shalt call his name John... And Zacharias said unto the angel, Whereby shall I know this? for I am an old man, and my wife well stricken in years. And the angel answering said unto him, I am Gabriel, that stand in the presence of God; and am sent to speak unto thee, and to shew thee these glad tidings. And, behold, thou shalt be dumb, and not able to speak, until the day that these things shall be performed, because thou believest not my words.

This is the first of four consecutive readings from Luke 1, which unfold the events leading up to Jesus' birth. It begins with the conception of John the Baptist, appropriately enough on this day, which is given the title 'O Root of Jesse'. John the Baptist's background emphasises the inheritance of the line that can be traced to King David, his father Jesse and beyond – as we saw two days ago. So we have the devout couple Zacharias and Elisabeth, who (like Joseph and Mary) seem highly qualified as parents because of their ancestry and personal faith.

But here the story looks back to another Old Testament tradition – that of the barren woman who has given up hope of children but goes on miraculously to bear a son. Elisabeth is in a line that includes Sarah, mother of Isaac, and Hannah, mother of the prophet Samuel. Yet the story behind John's birth gets more interesting than this, for it shows us all the dangers of simply resting on our tradition – like the crowds who later flocked to John's preaching in the desert. They claimed Abraham for their ancestor and thought that was enough, as if they didn't have to bother with anything like repentance or decent behaviour (Luke 3:8). So Zacharias dutifully performed his work in the temple in Jerusalem, but didn't expect anything to happen; he didn't seem to believe that God would really do anything. Does this sound familiar to those of us who have been faithfully going to church all these years? The last thing we expect is any action from God.

Among other things, this surely suggests the need to make the tradition our own, and act upon it. This is something that the Jewish people are very much aware of, right down to our own century. When I was invited to a Passover celebration at a synagogue recently, I was struck by the way that the prayers referred to God's saving work in delivering his people from bondage in Egypt and went on to emphasise that we should continue to act on what God was showing us: we had been strangers in the land, so we must be generous to the strangers we meet today. These stories aren't just charming tales from the past: they have a purpose that we must apply to ourselves, right now.

Instead, all too often, we want to display a sturdy independence, relying on our own versions of faith or what we think of as our talents, and trying to keep God in a tidy little box. We desperately need to break out of our self-reliance and truly turn to God. George Herbert conveys something of this in his poem 'The Pearl', when he refers to his skills and pleasures, while all the time sensing that God is waiting with a love that goes beyond them all. He knows the ways of learning, of honour and of pleasure; he is only human. These may be gifts of God,

but we have to travel beyond them to the creator who
gave them, just as we have to travel beyond the mere
facts of our tradition to reach its source.

> *I know the ways of Learning; both the head*
> *And pipes that feed the press, and make it run...*
> *Both th' old discoveries, and the new-found seas,*
> *The stock and surplus, cause and history:*
> *All these stand open, or I have the keys:*
> > *Yet I love thee.*

> *I know the ways of Honour, what maintains*
> *The quick returns of courtesy and wit...*
> *How many drams of spirit there must be*
> *To sell my life unto my friends or foes:*
> > *Yet I love thee.*

> *I know the ways of Pleasure, the sweet strains,*
> *The lullings and the relishes of it;*
> *The propositions of hot blood and brains;*
> *What mirth and music mean...*
> *My stuff is flesh, not brass; my senses live,*
> *And grumble oft, that they have more in me*
> *Than he that curbs them, being but one to five:*
> > *Yet I love thee.*

I know all these, and have them in my hand:
Therefore not sealed, but with open eyes
I fly to thee, and fully understand
Both the main sale, and the commodities;
And at what rate and price I have thy love;
With all the circumstances that may move:
Yet through these labyrinths, not my grovelling wit,
But thy silk twist let down from heav'n to me,
Did both conduct and teach me, how by it
           To climb to thee.

So George Herbert flies to God with open eyes, but it is God's silk thread, through the labyrinth of life, that enables him to find his way.

For prayer

Father, help me to climb to you, making your ways, your tradition, my own, and not resting in the distraction of your gifts.

20 December (O Key of David)

Luke 1:28–32a, 34–35a, 37–38 (KJV)

The mind-blowing paradoxes of God

And the angel came in unto [Mary], and said, Hail, thou that art highly favoured, the Lord is with thee: blessed art thou among women. And when she saw him, she was troubled at his saying, and cast in her mind what manner of salutation this should be. And the angel said unto her, Fear not, Mary: for thou hast found favour with God. And, behold, thou shalt conceive in thy womb, and bring forth a son, and shalt call his name Jesus. He shall be great, and shall be called the Son of the Highest… Then said Mary unto the angel, How shall this be, seeing I know not a man? And the angel answered and said unto her, The Holy Ghost shall come upon thee… For with God nothing shall be impossible. And Mary said, Behold the handmaid of the Lord; be it unto me according to thy word.

Here is a very different annunciation from the one that heralded John the Baptist's birth in yesterday's reading. As so often at this time of year, we have to jolt ourselves out of the beguiling familiarity of the words and the stories, which can so easily wash over us, leaving very little sense of what they are really about. This is where poets can help, in lending us fresh eyes and minds to give us new ideas about why it all matters. The imaginative connections they make can foster a deeper appreciation of God's actions.

W.H. Auden, in another section of *For the Time Being* (which we looked at two days ago), emphasises God's love and Mary's choice, leading us into a fuller sense of his providence. The poet imagines the angel Gabriel noting Mary's child-like playing of 'a dream of love':

> *Love wills your dream to happen, so*
> *Love's will on earth may be, through you,*
> *No longer a pretend but true.*

This is like yesterday's reading about making the story, the dream, our own: we can make it true and make it happen, right now. It stops being just a tale from the past and begins to influence us in the present.

Gabriel goes on to compare the choices made by Adam and Eve with the choice he is presenting to Mary:

> *… child, it lies*
> *Within your power of choosing to*
> *Conceive the Child who chooses you.*

God has chosen Mary, who has the opportunity to respond freely; she can say no, and, if she does, God will have to search out another means to be born on earth.

This sense of meditating on a cosmic pattern can be traced back to much earlier poets whom Auden would have read, such as the authors of anonymous medieval English lyrics and, in the 17th century, John Donne. In a poem from the early 14th century ('Gabriel, from heaven's king'), for example, the grand cosmic sweep is placed side by side with the domestic detail of what will happen to Mary. Gabriel explains to the baffled girl that the human race will be redeemed by her childbearing and brought out of torment:

> *All mankind will be ibought*
> *Through thy sweet childinge*
> *And out of pain ibrought.*

So it happened that Jesus, True God ('Soth God') was enclosed ('beloken') in her womb:

> *In her was Christ beloken, anon*
> *Soth God, Soth Man, in flesh and bone.*

Following on from this, three centuries later, Donne's sonnet 'Annunciation' famously ends with the line 'Immensity cloistered in thy dear womb', which he goes on to use as the first line of another sonnet, making part of a sequence of seven poems under the title 'La Corona' ('The Crown'). Donne builds up to this point by addressing Mary and exploring the paradoxes of the Son of God's coming to earth. He 'cannot sin, and yet all sins must bear' and 'cannot die, yet cannot choose but die'. God has been planning his coming since before the beginning of time and is prepared to be limited to the prison of her womb:

> *Ere by the spheres time was created, thou*
> *Wast in His mind, who is thy Son and Brother;*
> *Whom thou conceiv'st, conceived; yea thou art now*
> *Thy Maker's maker, and thy Father's mother;*
> *Thou hast light in dark, and shut'st in little room,*
> *Immensity cloistered in thy dear womb.*

With such mind-blowing ideas, often we can make only a feeble attempt to hold them in our minds and contemplate their wonder. But, knowing that God is Lord over it all, we can also rejoice in the play of paradox and intricate patterning of ideas, such as 'Thy Maker's maker, and thy Father's mother'. It's all part of the richness of God's gifts, which draws us on to worship him.

For prayer

Heavenly Father, who chose the Blessed Virgin Mary to be the mother of the promised saviour: fill us your servants with your grace, that in all things we may embrace your holy will and with her rejoice in your salvation; through Jesus Christ our Lord. Amen

Post-Communion Prayer for the Fourth Sunday of Advent, Common Worship

21 December (O Dayspring)

Luke 1:39–45 (KJV)

In praise of Mary

And Mary arose in those days, and went into the hill country with haste, into a city of Juda; And entered into the house of Zacharias, and saluted Elisabeth. And it came to pass, that, when Elisabeth heard the salutation of Mary, the babe leaped in her womb; and Elisabeth was filled with the Holy Ghost: And she spake out with a loud voice, and said, Blessed art thou among women, and blessed is the fruit of thy womb. And whence is this to me, that the mother of my Lord should come to me? For, lo, as soon as the voice of thy salutation sounded in mine ears, the babe leaped in my womb for joy. And blessed is she that believed: for there shall be a performance of those things which were told her from the Lord.

In these verses, which follow straight on from yesterday's reading, we see the consequences of Mary's decision. We are plunged immediately into the next stage of the story as Mary goes 'with haste' to visit her cousin Elisabeth. There is a sense of needing to get away quickly, perhaps to avoid the scandal brewing up over her extra-marital pregnancy. Today may be designated 'O Dayspring', or 'Dawn', in the Advent antiphons, but the dawning of a new age begins in the messy reality of malicious gossip and hurried travel arrangements.

At least here Mary is guaranteed a welcome, although Luke isn't concerned to emphasise the warmth of human companionship or female solidarity. What he emphasises is Mary's significance in terms of the history of salvation: this is where we hear about the new dawn. She is blessed and the mother of 'my Lord', declares Elisabeth, whose use of the word 'Lord' rather than 'Christ' or 'Messiah' also suggests Jesus' rule over all the world, rather than just his leadership of the chosen people. Elisabeth welcomes him on behalf of everyone.

Some commentators have extrapolated medical arguments about foetal development from the idea of the baby John the Baptist leaping in his mother's womb, but surely the real significance is that those who have been chosen and specially touched by God – both John and his mother Elisabeth – recognise and acknowledge the mother of the Saviour. Mary may have been isolated in many ways, especially from her own community, but what she is doing is welcomed at least by these two relatives.

Elisabeth's words, 'Blessed art thou among women, and blessed is the fruit of thy womb', have been taken up to form a central part of the 'Hail Mary':

Hail Mary, full of grace, the Lord is with thee; blessed art thou among women, and blessed is the fruit of thy womb, Jesus. Holy Mary, Mother of God, pray for us sinners, now and at the hour of our death. Amen

This traditional prayer, whose origins lie in the medieval period, is used by Catholics in the rosary, as well as often at the end of intercessions in church. Other traditions have steered clear of it, frightened by the dangers of seeming to promote Mary above her son, but I have heard it justified as being very biblical and a simple request for prayer from one person to another. Once I heard it described as a combination of two Bible verses (Luke 1:28, 'Hail...', and verse 42, 'Blessed art thou...'), followed by a prayerful hymn: 'Holy Mary... pray for us...' It's definitely not a prayer to Mary (as some have mistakenly assumed it to be), but a request for her to pray for us, yet many Christians still aren't comfortable with the idea. The idea of asking anyone from the distant past to pray for us can seem odd, or even unhealthy.

Poets can sidestep such controversy, though, by being able to address Mary imaginatively, in their own private way, rather than in public prayers in church. This does not mean that they leave their intellectual and theological senses behind when they write: far from it, as they encourage a deeper engagement with the ideas that form our faith. But they are freer to meditate on the possibilities of various aspects of the Bible story, including both theological ideas about salvation and the human dimensions of the events being described.

So Elisabeth's praise of Mary is echoed in many medieval poems, such as the one below from the 13th century, which foster a sense of the wonder of what God did with and in her. Such writing expands our sympathies and gives us a larger notion of God's love and our part in it. Like the 'Hail Mary', it brings together both praise of Mary and people's hopes and fears for their own death. It also reminds me of the way Mary is sometimes pictured as 'Mater misericordia' (merciful mother), sheltering people under her cloak.

> Lady, I thank thee,
>   With heart so milde. [gracious]
> For the good that thou hast done me
>   With thine sweet child.

Thou art good and sweet and bright,
Of all others icoren. [chosen]
Of thee was that sweet wight, [creature]
That was Jesus, iboren. [born]

Maiden milde, bidd I thee [I pray thee]
With thy sweet child,
That thou herdie [shelter] me
To have God's milce. [mercy]

Mother, look on me,
With thine sweet eye,
Rest and bliss give thou me,
My lady, when I die.

For prayer

Mighty God, by whose grace Elizabeth rejoiced
with Mary and greeted her as the mother of the
Lord: look with favour on your lowly servants
that, with Mary, we may magnify your holy name
and rejoice to acclaim her Son our Saviour, who
is alive and reigns with you, in the unity of the
Holy Spirit, one God, now and for ever. Amen

Collect for the Visitation of the Blessed Virgin Mary to Elizabeth
(31 May), Common Worship

❧ Week 4 ❧

'That holy thing'

At last, in the fourth week, we reach Christmas Day itself, after all the prophecies, the build-up of expectations and the thoughts about what it might all mean – not to mention the frantic present-buying and preparation for entertaining people. So, this week, we have the last two Advent antiphons, the joy of the birth itself, and then we are plunged immediately back into the suffering that is inevitable in life, remembering the martyrdom of St Stephen and of the Holy Innocents.

The poets who accompany us through this roller-coaster journey reflect on the mind-boggling immensity of God's choosing to come and be limited by his creation, and on our response – feeble though it may be. So we move from John Donne's famous 'Immensity cloistered in thy dear womb' to Ben Jonson's question, 'Can man forget the story?' As ever, what matters most is our answer to this question, right now.

22 December (O King of the Nations)

Luke 1:46–56 (BCP)

Spring on the shortest day

My soul doth magnify the Lord: and my spirit hath rejoiced in God my Saviour. For he hath regarded: the lowliness of his hand-maiden. For behold, from hence-forth: all generations shall call me blessed. For he that is mighty hath magnified me: and holy is his Name. And his mercy is on them that fear him: throughout all generations. He hath shewed strength with his arm: he hath scattered the proud in the imagination of their hearts. He hath put down the mighty from their seat: and hath exalted the humble and meek. He hath filled the hungry with good things: and the rich he hath sent empty away. He remembering his mercy hath holpen his servant Israel: as he promised to our forefathers, Abraham and his seed for ever.

Again, following straight on from yesterday's reading, here is Mary's outpouring of praise. Her words look back to earlier thanksgivings by women who are unexpect-edly promised motherhood, most obviously Hannah, the mother of Samuel (1 Samuel 2:1–10). Hannah begins,

'My heart rejoiceth in the Lord' and continues with simi-lar themes to Mary's – about the reversal of the usual worldly order of human strength ('The bows of the mighty men are broken, and they that stumbled are girded with strength', v. 4, and 'He raiseth up the poor out of the dust', v. 8).

Both Mary and Hannah celebrate the faith and ultimate triumph of the devout poor, who are rewarded by God while the rich and powerful are 'sent empty away'. Those who are proud in the imagination of their hearts have been deceived by their wealth. They have trusted in God's gifts rather than God himself, and their self-sufficiency has led them astray. One of the many echoes of this all-too-modern phenomenon can be seen in India, even today. A larger proportion of the Dalit community, those at the bottom of the pile (the former 'Untouchables'), who are left to carry out the grimmest work, have embraced Christianity than those from other sections of society. They can see that it offers hope when so many worldly interests are stacked against them.

Also, appropriately for the day of the antiphon 'O King of the Nations', this song of triumph places Mary way beyond her sphere of lowly, humdrum life, waiting to get married in a backwater of a remote province of the Roman empire. Instead, it promotes her to the grand sweep of history, in which all generations will call her blessed, and puts her with the newly exalted mighty ones and the holiest of the chosen people.

Today is also significant in terms of the whole course of the year, being the shortest day (in the northern hemisphere). This is, of course, the reason we celebrate Christmas around now, having taken over the various pre-Christian festivals of light and the dying year. The annunciation and Jesus' miraculous conception are set in spring, at the time of new life, but the birth happens at the darkest time of the year. It doesn't get any gloomier than this, yet it is out of the deepest darkness that hope springs. The year is about to turn. There is a sense of being on the brink.

Robert Herrick (1591–1674) touches on this interplay between spring and Christmas in the lyrics of a Christmas carol that he wrote for a number of voices to sing. Here, the Saviour's birth brings a new spring, right in the middle of winter: he 'turns all the patient ground to flowers':

Voice 1: *Dark and dull night, fly hence away,*
And give the honour to this Day,
That sees December turn'd to May.

Voice 2: *If we may ask the reason, say:*
The why, and wherefore all things here
Seem like the spring-time of the year?

Voice 3: *Why does the chilling Winter's morn*
Smile, like a field beset with corn?
Or smell, like to a mead new-shorn,
Thus, on the sudden?

Voice 4: *Come and see*
The cause, why things thus fragrant be:
'Tis He is born, whose quick'ning Birth
Gives life and luster, public mirth,
To Heaven and the under-Earth.

Chorus: *We see Him come, and know Him ours,*
Who, with His sunshine, and His showers,
Turns all the patient ground to flowers.

Voice 1: *The Darling of the world is come,*
And fit it is we find a room
To welcome Him.

Voice 2: *The nobler part*
Of all the house here, is the Heart,

Chorus: *Which we will give Him; and bequeath*
This holly and this ivy wreath,
To do Him honour who's our King,
And Lord of all this revelling.

From 'A Christmas Carol, Sung to the King in the Presence
at White Hall'

Crucially, Herrick homes in on the purpose of all this
'revelling' – the need for us all to ask Christ into our hearts.
'And fit it is we find a room / To welcome Him.'

For reflection

As we stand on the brink of Christmas, at the darkest time of
the year, perhaps feeling overwhelmed by frantic prepara-
tions, is it possible to pause for a moment and think about
what God has done for each one of us in Jesus? Can we do
anything, even at this late stage, to prepare our heart to
find a room to welcome him?

23 December (O Emmanuel)

Hebrews 10:5–10 (NRSV)

'Let me go there'

Consequently, when Christ came into the world, he said, 'Sacrifices and offerings you have not desired, but a body you have prepared for me; in burnt-offerings and sin-offerings you have taken no pleasure. Then I said, "See, God, I have come to do your will, O God" (in the scroll of the book it is written of me).' When he said above, 'You have neither desired nor taken pleasure in sacrifices and offerings and burnt-offerings and sin-offerings' (these are offered according to the law), then he added, 'See, I have come to do your will.' He abolishes the first in order to establish the second. And it is by God's will that we have been sanctified through the offering of the body of Jesus Christ once for all.

Today we disrupt the sequence of readings from Luke 1 to think about why the birth of Christ is happening. This passage, which has been set by the church for today, seems to be focusing on the question in a fairly oblique way, thrusting us into a sphere of theological complexities.

At least, though, we can immediately hear the repeated emphasis on doing God's will.

Working back from this basic message, the preceding verses in the letter to the Hebrews examine the contrast between the old law, with its sacrifices of bulls and goats, which had to be repeated each year, and the new dispensation of Christ. The law couldn't make worshippers perfect, but its sacrifices were 'an annual reminder of sins' (Hebrews 10:3, NIV). So, here, Christ abolishes the continual round of animal sacrifices in order to establish the primacy of God's will. He sets up the idea of obeying God's will as the most important thing any of us can do, taking precedence over every other religious action (such as all those other sacrifices and offerings).

It is through Jesus' offering of himself – his obedience to the Father's will – that we are sanctified and made holy. The NIV translates part of verse 7 as 'Here I am... I have come to do your will.' So Jesus volunteers freely, as the young Samuel did, and many others before him: 'Here am I... Speak; for thy servant heareth' (1 Samuel 3:4, 10, KJV). Of course, we too can become part of this tradition in our own way. We are all free to do God's will.

There is a moving portrayal of Jesus' obedience in a poem called 'The Coming' by R.S. Thomas (1913–2000), the Welsh poet and priest. He takes the cosmic setting that we have seen used by other writers (such as the anonymous medieval poet whose work we read on 20 December) and imagines God the Father and God the Son planning the incarnation, showing their tender love and compassion for the world, which is depicted as a bare place where the people hold out their thin arms.

And God held in his hand
A small globe. Look, he said.
The son looked. Far off,
As through water, he saw
A scorched land of fierce
Colour. The light burned
There; crusted buildings
Cast their shadows; a bright
Serpent, a river
Uncoiled itself, radiant
With slime.
                On a bare
Hill a bare tree saddened
The sky. Many people
Held out their thin arms
To it, as though waiting
For a vanished April
To return to its crossed
Boughs. The son watched
Them. Let me go there, he said.

This is truly Emmanuel, 'God is with us' – as today's antiphon, 'O Emmanuel' (the last of the seven) suggests. The Son of God chooses to come and be with us. Father, Son and Holy Spirit love us so much that they want to be alongside us. Even if we have been squeezed hard by the rounds of carol services, present-buying and food preparation, there is still time to pray that we might be ready to welcome Christ here and offer ourselves to him in return.

The following prayer by Jeremy Taylor (1613–67) gathers several of these themes, together with the important Advent emphasis on death and heaven, as part of a renewed dedication to God.

For prayer

> Most holy and eternal God, lord and sovereign of
> all the creatures, I humbly present to thy divine
> majesty, myself, my soul and body, my thoughts
> and my words, my actions and intentions, my
> passions and my sufferings, to be disposed
> by thee to thy glory; to be blessed by thy
> providence; to be guided by thy counsel; to be
> sanctified by thy Spirit; and afterwards that my
> body and soul may be received into glory;

for nothing can perish which is under thy
custody, and the enemy of souls cannot devour,
what is thy portion, nor take it out of thy hands.
This day, O Lord, and all the days of my life,
I dedicate to thy honour, and the actions of my
calling to the uses of grace, and the religion
of all my days to be united to the merits and
intercession of my holy Saviour, Jesus; that,
in him and for him, I may be pardoned and
accepted.

24 December (Christmas Eve)

Luke 1:68–79 (BCP)

An answer to our deepest needs

Blessed be the Lord God of Israel: for he hath visited, and redeemed his people; And hath raised up a mighty salvation for us: in the house of his servant David; As he spake by the mouth of his holy Prophets: which have been since the world began; That we should be saved from our enemies: and from the hands of all that hate us; To perform the mercy promised to our forefathers: and to remember his holy covenant; To perform the oath which he sware to our forefather Abraham: that he would give us; That we being delivered out of the hands of our enemies: might serve him without fear; In holiness and righteousness before him: all the days of our life. And thou, child, shalt be called the Prophet of the Highest: for thou shalt go before the face of the Lord to prepare his ways; To give knowledge of salvation unto his people: for the remission of their sins; Through the tender mercy of our God: whereby the day-spring from on high hath visited us; To give light to them that sit in darkness, and in the shadow of death: and to guide our feet into the way of peace.

Here, on the very brink of the great festival, one of the passages set by the church for the day is another outpouring of praise – one of the most touching. Zechariah, the father of John the Baptist, is at last able to speak after having been struck dumb, and does so in the words of this prophecy. (When he addresses 'thou, child' towards the end, he is referring to his son.) Like Mary in the Magnificat, Zechariah emphasises God's action in saving his chosen people from those who have worldly power. God will redeem his people and, to prepare for this redemption, he will send his prophet, John, to tell them how they can be saved by repenting of their sins.

God has done this, so now, as we saw yesterday, it is up to us to respond and (as we also saw the day before, on 22 December) to welcome him. We can hold in our minds this inheritance of the promises God made to his people, as we retell the stories of Mary and Joseph arriving in Bethlehem, and think how we can bring them into our own lives.

Sir John Suckling (1609–42), a near-contemporary of Robert Herrick, takes further Herrick's image of greeting the Lord ('we find a room / To welcome Him') in a deft short poem entitled 'Upon Christ His Birth' (reprinted in full below). It looks to the purpose of Christ's coming, which will be meaningless unless we are able to allow

him to enter our empty hearts. Despite the 'too much fullness' in Bethlehem, there is space ('some want' or lack)
for him. We can let Jesus come and find lodging with us.

Strange news! a city full? will none give way
To lodge a guest that comes not every day?
No inn, nor tavern void? yet I descry
One empty place alone, where we may lie:
In too much fullness is some want: but where?
Men's empty hearts: let's ask for lodging there.
But if they not admit us, then we'll say
Their hearts, as well as inns, are made of clay.

Centuries earlier, St Augustine of Hippo (354–430) also
compared people to buildings. In his *Confessions*, the
book tracing the growth of his faith, he prays to God,
'My soul is like a house… it is in ruins, but I ask you to
remake it' (I.5). Later on, he cries out, 'What can save us
but your hand, remaking what you have made?' (V.7). And,
of course, one of the most famous parts of his spiritual
autobiography comes at the very beginning, where he
declares to God, 'You have made us for yourself, and our
hearts are restless until they rest in you' (I.1).

When Christ comes to live with us and in us, he will
become the one 'in whom all our hungers are satisfied'
(as it says in the Common Worship Holy Communion

service). George MacDonald (1824–1905) conveys this idea in a tender but telling way, in his poem 'That Holy Thing'. Christ does not conform to our selfish expectations about making ourselves feel bigger, but comes down his own 'secret stair' to answer our real, deeper needs.

They all were looking for a king
  To slay their foes, and lift them high:
Thou cam'st, a little baby thing
  That made a woman cry.

O Son of Man, to right my lot
  Naught but Thy presence can avail;
Yet on the road Thy wheels are not,
  Nor on the sea Thy sail!

My how or when Thou wilt not heed,
  But come down Thine own secret stair,
That Thou mayst answer all my need –
  Yea, every bygone prayer.

This is surely the message that we need to communicate to all those who come to church, today and tomorrow, as they have come to carol services throughout this season. It may be the only time in the year when they set foot in church, but they ought to be able to hear from us how God has the power to satisfy them more than can the money, respect and beauty that we all seek in God's gifts. Only God himself can fill the aching void; even human love is only a reflection of his fierce, burning love, which is the source of it all.

For reflection

If someone were to ask you today (which they might), 'So what's Christmas meant to mean?', would you have an answer? Could you plan what you might say?

25 December (Christmas Day)

Luke 2:7–14 (KJV)

'Each of us his lamb will bring'

And [Mary] brought forth her firstborn son, and wrapped him in swaddling clothes, and laid him in a manger; because there was no room for them in the inn. And there were in the same country shepherds abiding in the field, keeping watch over their flock by night. And, lo, the angel of the Lord came upon them, and the glory of the Lord shone round about them: and they were sore afraid. And the angel said unto them, Fear not: for, behold, I bring you good tidings of great joy, which shall be to all people. For unto you is born this day in the city of David a Saviour, which is Christ the Lord. And this shall be a sign unto you; Ye shall find the babe wrapped in swaddling clothes, lying in a manger. And suddenly there was with the angel a multitude of the heavenly host praising God, and saying, Glory to God in the highest, and on earth peace, good will toward men.

After all the build-up, here at last is Jesus' birth. In common with many poets and others, during Advent we can relish the value of God's quiet preparations, but now we need to take time to ponder the nativity itself. In the poem below, which follows on directly in a sequence from the one about the annunciation that we read on 20 December, John Donne appreciates God's intention in deliberately limiting himself and making himself weak in order to come into our world to save humankind:

> Immensity cloistered in thy dear womb,
> Now leaves his well-belov'd imprisonment,
> There he hath made himself to his intent
> Weak enough, now into our world to come...
> See'st thou, my soul, with thy faith's eyes, how he
> Which fills all place, yet none holds him, doth lie?
> Was not his pity towards thee wondrous high...?
> 'Nativity'

This poem gives us somewhere to start from, so that we can spend a while in praise at God's amazing gift, which might otherwise overwhelm us. Praise and adoration are always a vital part of any prayer life, although it can seem all too easy to skip over them. If we think of the structure for one popular way of praying, ACTS (adoration, confession, thanksgiving and supplication), we can see how they should be the starting point. Indeed, most of us are surely capable of making some kind of adoration our first thought on waking. Even when anxieties for the coming day creep in, we can at least try to spare some time to get a sense of perspective, in which to set before ourselves the real purpose for which God created us: to praise and love him.

Hymns, carols and poems (such as the one below by Richard Crashaw) can be helpful spurs here. Crashaw echoes something of Donne's 'immensity cloistered' in his line 'Eternity shut in a span!' as well as teasing out those paradoxes that we have seen elsewhere about how wondrous it is that earth and heaven meet together at the birth of Christ. He also rejoices in the reversal of the usual order of the world that Mary celebrated in the Magnificat, when he praises the shepherds for their clean hands (presumably not literally) and clear hearts.

Welcome to our wond'ring sight
   Eternity shut in a span!
Summer in winter! Day in night!
   Heaven in earth! and God in man!
Great little one, whose glorious Birth,
Lifts earth to heaven, stoops heaven to earth…

Welcome, (though not to those gay flies
  Guilded i'th' beams of earthly kings
Slippery souls in smiling eyes)
But to poor Shepherds, simple things,
  That use no varnish, no oil'd arts,
But lift clean hands full of clear hearts…

To thee meek majesty, soft king
  Of simple graces, and sweet loves,
Each of us his lamb will bring,
  Each his pair of silver doves.
At last, in fire of thy fair eyes,
We'll burn, our own best sacrifice.

From 'A Hymn of the Nativity, Sung by the Shepherds'

When this swirling cosmic adoration becomes over-whelming, the poet leads us gently towards a simple, direct response: 'Each of us his lamb will bring.' We all have something to offer. There is some response we can each make – whether a kindness or an act of charity or forbearance (perhaps particularly the latter, if we are thrust into family gatherings at this time of year).

One medieval poet, for example, imagines Mary nurtur-ing Jesus but fearing that she hasn't got enough to give him (not 'clout nor cloth'). She laments her poor offer-ings (only a cattle stall as a cradle, and with animals for companions); yet she still realises that she can help to protect him, from the cold at least.

> *Jesu, sweet son dear,*
> *On poorful bed liest thou here,*
>> *And that me grieveth sore;*
> *For thy cradle is as a bere, [cattle stall]*
> *Ox and ass be thy fere: [companions]*
>> *Weep I may therefore.*
>
> *Jesu, sweet, be not wroth,*
> *Though I n'ave clout nor cloth*
>> *Thee on for to fold, [enfold]*
> *Thee on to fold nor to wrap,*
> *For I n'ave clout nor lap; [fold of a garment]*
> *But lay thou thy feet to my pap*
>> *And wite thee from the cold. [protect thee]*
>
> Anonymous (late 14th century)

For prayer

Father God, help me to realise that even my feeble gifts can be offered to you in honest love. Amen

26 December (St Stephen)

Acts 7:51, 53–60 (NRSV)

The sweep of the season from joy to sadness

'You stiff-necked people, uncircumcised in heart and ears, you are for ever opposing the Holy Spirit, just as your ancestors used to do... You are the ones that received the law as ordained by angels, and yet you have not kept it.' When they heard these things, they became enraged and ground their teeth at Stephen. But filled with the Holy Spirit, he gazed into heaven and saw the glory of God and Jesus standing at the right hand of God. 'Look,' he said, 'I see the heavens opened and the Son of Man standing at the right hand of God!' But they covered their ears, and with a loud shout all rushed together against him. Then they dragged him out of the city and began to stone him; and the witnesses laid their coats at the feet of a young man named Saul. While they were stoning Stephen, he prayed, 'Lord Jesus, receive my spirit.' Then he knelt down and cried out in a loud voice, 'Lord, do not hold this sin against them.' When he had said this, he died.

It always seems strange to me that the church marks the feast of St Stephen, the first martyr, right after the joy of Christmas Day – but, of course, it does make sense in a broader way. Alongside the joy is the suffering. Neither celebrations nor laments exist in isolation: both are essential and inevitable elements in our life. What is more, there is often something about the way we celebrate Christmas that can make us feel more aware of sadness, because of the contrast with the joy that we think we are supposed to feel. When it seems as if everyone else is having a great time with family and friends, some people are always going to feel left out, remembering happier times from the past. We're also more likely at this season to recall the people we miss from earlier years.

Today is the second day in the season of Christmas, which lasts until Candlemas, which is also called the feast of the Presentation of Christ in the Temple, on 2 February. This festival marks the time when the six-week-old Jesus was taken to the temple in Jerusalem, in accordance with the Jewish Law. It was there that he was greeted by Anna and Simeon (Luke 2:22–38). Today may be the end of Christmas for shops and the rest of the secular world, but for Christians it is only the beginning.

One early poem that encompasses the whole sweep of the season is an anonymous lyric from the early 15th century. It works through the various festivals that are marked at this time of year: Christmas Day, St Stephen's Day (where it refers to the Bible passage above), St John the Evangelist's Day (where it mentions John, the disciple Jesus loved, who took Mary into his care when Jesus was on the cross), the Holy Innocents, St Thomas Becket, the Circumcision (on 1 January, when Jesus was named and circumcised at eight days old, in accordance with the Old Testament covenant between God and his people – in the poem below, this is seen as his submitting to the requirements of the law, as an example of meekness), the Epiphany, and finally the Presentation in the Temple. Crucially, the poem sets them all in the context of the celebration of Christ and the purpose of all these saints in witnessing to him in front of the world. It suggests how all these varied characters and events can be enfolded in God's care, even after all the suffering they encompass (or, indeed, like the Holy Innocents, who get a mention only as a result of their suffering), because they suffered for Christ.

> *Make we mirth*
> *For Christ's birth,*
> *And sing we Yule till Candlemas.*

The first day of Yule have we in mind
How God was man born of our kind,
For he the bonds would unbind
Of all our sins and wickedness.

The second day we sing of Stephen,
That stoned was, and steyed up even
   [ascended directly]
To God that he saw stood in Heaven,
And crowned was for his prowess.

The third day longeth to St John, [belongs to]
That was Christ's darling, dearer none,
Whom he betook, when he should gon, [go]
His mother dear for her cleanness. [purity]

The fourth day of the children young
That Herod to death had do with wrong.
   [put to death]
And Christ they could none tell with tongue,
But with their blood bear him witness.

The fifth day longeth to St Thomas,
That as a strong pillar of brass,
Held up the Church and slain he was,
For he stood with righteousness.

The eighth day took Jesu his name,
That saved mankind from sin and shame,
And circumcised was for no blame
But for ensample of meekness.

The twelfth day offered to him kings three
Gold, myrrh and cence, these gifts free: [noble gifts]
For God and man and King was he,
Thus they worshipped his worthiness.

On the fortieth day came Mary mild
Unto the temple with her child
To show her clean that never was filed, [defiled]
And therewith endeth Christmas.

The poem doesn't mention Stephen's great long speech to the Sanhedrin (the end of which is included at the beginning of today's Bible passage), which precipitated his being driven out and stoned to death. Instead, it focuses on the conclusion of the story – Stephen's being crowned in heaven as a martyr. It is as if the poet cares only for the ultimate effect.

As we have already seen, it's always the reasons and purposes of God that matter, not the supposedly religious acts with which we so often try to fob him off. It is the spirit that is important, not the letter of the law, for God dwells not in temples made with hands (Acts 7:48); he is spirit, and we worship him in spirit and in truth (John 4:24). This is why we need to repent of being 'stiff-necked people, uncircumcised in heart and ears, [who] are for ever opposing the Holy Spirit' (Acts 7:51).

It's a message that we need to keep bringing to mind, even among the mince pies and torn wrapping paper of today.

For prayer

Father in heaven, thank you for this season of Christmas, with its joys, its memories and its saints who honoured you even in their suffering. Help us to turn back to you in the midst of all that is happening around us. Amen

27 December (St John the Evangelist)

John 21:19b–25 (NRSV)

The priority of loving one another

After this [Jesus] said to [Peter], 'Follow me.' Peter turned and saw the disciple whom Jesus loved following them; he was the one who had reclined next to Jesus at the supper and had said, 'Lord, who is it that is going to betray you?' When Peter saw him, he said to Jesus, 'Lord, what about him?' Jesus said to him, 'If it is my will that he remain until I come, what is that to you? Follow me!' So the rumour spread in the community that this disciple would not die. Yet Jesus did not say to him that he would not die, but, 'If it is my will that he remain until I come, what is that to you?' This is the disciple who is testifying to these things and has written them, and we know that his testimony is true. But there are also many other things that Jesus did; if every one of them were written down, I suppose that the world itself could not contain the books that would be written.

As we found yesterday with Stephen, after the drama of Christmas Day we are plunged in again with the more everyday concerns of following Jesus. So now we celebrate the feast of St John the Evangelist, who is traditionally seen as the author of the fourth gospel as well as three epistles and the book of Revelation (though many scholars question most particularly the last one). This is John, the 'disciple whom Jesus loved', usually thought of as a young man who, with Peter and James, saw Jesus on the mountain at the transfiguration and was next to him at the last supper.

There is a well-established tradition that John later settled in Ephesus and lived to the age of 94, the last of the twelve apostles. Jerome tells a story of how, when John was old and becoming frail, he would be carried down to the gathering of Christians and would tell them: 'My little children, love one another.' When they asked why he kept repeating this, he replied, 'Because it is the word of the Lord, and if you keep it, you are doing enough.' The message 'Love one another' certainly does crop up repeatedly in the three epistles of John. See 1 John 4:7, for example: 'Dear friends, let us love one another, for love comes from God' (NIV).

This sense of 'doing enough' has a modern ring to it, like the idea of being a 'good enough parent'. We shouldn't be too harsh on ourselves if we are not perfect parents, as our children are almost certainly getting enough of what they need. We don't need to be brilliant at everything, but perhaps, if we try to love each other, as John recommends, that will be sufficient for most purposes. This can be an immense comfort when we think how woefully inadequate we are being as parents (or, indeed, as friends, sons or daughters), especially in comparison with others who seem to have the energy and imagination to do much more exciting things with their children and in their other relationships.

Being 'good enough' is certainly better than the rubber-necking, almost prurient obsession with others that Peter indulges in during his conversation with Jesus on the beach: 'Lord, what about him?' (v. 21). There are echoes here of Jesus' parable of the labourers in the vineyard, where the landowner has sharp words for those who are bothered about the amount that others are being paid, ignoring the terms on which they have themselves been hired. 'I am not being unfair to you, friend. Didn't you agree to work for a denarius?... Or are you envious because I am generous?' he says (Matthew 20:13, 15, NIV).

This fits in with the need to get our priorities right, which the overarching message of 'Love one another' conveys. Some Christmas poems share this sense of putting in order what is most vital. It echoes the stress on God's purposes and the need for our response, which we have seen in a number of poets already. Ben Jonson (1572–1637), for example, emphasises the salvation that Christ's birth brings about. The creator of heaven and earth limited himself to a manger in order to win us.

The Son of God, th' eternal king,
That did us all salvation bring,
   And freed the soul from danger;
He whom the whole world could not take,
The Word, which heaven and earth did make,
   Was now laid in a manger…

What comfort by him do we win,
Who made himself the price of sin,
   To make us heirs of glory?
To see this babe, all innocence;
A martyr born in our defence:
   Can man forget this story?
From 'A Hymn on the Nativity of My Saviour'

This is a story we can be confident in telling others. It reflects the most celebrated part of John the Evangelist's writing, the prologue to his gospel, where his sense of right priorities predominates, and he stresses the need for our response: 'In the beginning was the Word, and the Word was with God, and the Word was God... And the Word was made flesh, and dwelt among us, (and we beheld his glory, the glory as of the only begotten of the Father,) full of grace and truth' (John 1:1, 14, KJV).

For prayer

Merciful Lord, cast your bright beams of light upon the Church: that, being enlightened by the teaching of your blessed apostle and evangelist Saint John, we may so walk in the light of your truth that we may at last attain to the light of everlasting life; through Jesus Christ your incarnate Son our Lord. Amen

Collect for St John, Apostle and Evangelist, Common Worship

28 December (Holy Innocents)

Matthew 2:13–18 (KJV)

'When wretches have their will'

And when they were departed, behold, the angel of the Lord appeareth to Joseph in a dream, saying, Arise, and take the young child and his mother, and flee into Egypt, and be thou there until I bring thee word: for Herod will seek the young child to destroy him. When he arose, he took the young child and his mother by night, and departed into Egypt: And was there until the death of Herod: that it might be fulfilled which was spoken of the Lord by the prophet, saying, Out of Egypt have I called my son. Then Herod, when he saw that he was mocked of the wise men, was exceeding wroth, and sent forth, and slew all the children that were in Bethlehem, and in all the coasts thereof, from two years old and under, according to the time which he had diligently inquired of the wise men. Then was fulfilled that which was spoken by Jeremiah the prophet, saying, In Rama was there a voice heard, lamentation, and weeping, and great mourning, Rachel weeping for her children, and would not be comforted, because they are not.

The idea of sorrow at what should be a joyful time continues with a vengeance here, with the Massacre of the Innocents, the most chilling episode in the whole of the Christmas story. Matthew is surely right to refer to Jeremiah at this point: Rachel would not be comforted. There is no real comfort when you've buried your children. It goes against nature for them to die before you do. I think of all the mothers of young soldiers killed in Afghanistan, Iraq or elsewhere, whose boys never came home. We've seen the potent images of repatriation processions through Royal Wootton Bassett and Carterton, and of war memorials and cemeteries on Remembrance Sunday: the fathers, often strong men bowed down by grief; the young friends, tearful and unsure about what to do; the new widows, facing a bleak future without their other half; the old soldiers, medals gleaming on their chests, calling to mind their friends lost long ago but never forgotten. Even when we believe the cause of a war was just, part of us always wonders how it can have been allowed to happen.

With the Massacre of the Innocents, much of the answer is clear enough. Herod gave a straightforward order, which was carried out. He exercised his free will to be a tyrant and murdered anyone he perceived as a threat, even down to tiny babies. I have seen medieval mystery plays dramatising the scenes of this killing – soldiers rampaging gleefully with their spears and agonised mothers pleading with them and desperate to escape. Some versions seem to relish the horror, exploiting its extremity as if to balance out the joy and serenity of the nativity. One of my friends is from Coventry, where the city's own cycle of mystery plays is often performed. She refuses to go any more, after too many productions have eked out the trauma of this scene.

William Byrd's 'Lullaby: My sweet little baby' (1588) offers a similar way of looking at this part of the story. He puts the blame firmly with Herod: this is the woe that will come about 'when wretches have their will', as they have so often throughout history – from Herod to Attila the Hun, to Hitler, Stalin and Pol Pot. He imagines Mary singing to Jesus, though he has good reason to cry, as he is threatened with slaughter by the evil king. The last verse is addressed to Jesus, the one whose reign has been prophesied and whom no 'caitiffs' ('despicable cowards') can betray. Mary can celebrate the fact that, for now at least, the wretches have not been able to get their way. As we know, this isn't the whole story: those other mothers will still grieve and this baby, although he survives now, will grow up to be betrayed later in life. But there will be enough joy at the very end of the story.

Lulla, la lulla, lulla, lullaby
My sweet little baby, what meanest thou to cry?
Be still my blessed babe, though cause thou hast to
*   mourn,*
Whose blood most innocent to shed the cruel king
*   hath sworn:*
And lo, alas, behold what slaughters he doth make,
Shedding the blood of infants all, sweet Saviour, for
*   thy sake.*
A King is born, they say, which King this king would
*   kill.*
O woe, and woeful heavy day, when wretches have
*   their will! ...*

But thou shalt live and reign as Sibyls have
*   foresayed,*
As all the prophets prophesy, whose mother, yet
*   a maid*
And perfect virgin pure, with her breasts shall
*   upbreed*
Both God and man, that all hath made, the Son of
*   heavenly seed,*
Whom caitiffs none can 'tray, whom tyrants none
*   can kill.*
O joy, and joyful happy day, when wretches want
*   [lack] their will.*

Another poem, much shorter and sweeter, seeks comfort in the delights awaiting the baby martyrs when they get to heaven. They will join in the saints' chorus, learning to sing even before they learnt to speak on earth. There will be an infants' paradise for them.

Go smiling souls, your new-built cages break,
In Heaven you'll learn to sing ere here to speak,
Nor let the milky fonts that bathe your thirst,
Be your delay;
The place that calls you hence, is at the worst
Milk all the way.

Richard Crashaw, 'To the Infant Martyrs'

For prayer

Heavenly Father, whose children suffered at
the hands of Herod, though they had done no
wrong: by the suffering of your Son and by the
innocence of our lives frustrate all evil designs
and establish your reign of justice and peace;
through Jesus Christ your Son our Lord. Amen

Collect for the Holy Innocents, Common Worship

🎴 Week 5 🎴

Back to the new life

This is the last of our weeks of readings, and it has two extra days attached at the end, which take us up to the Epiphany on 6 January. We move from the last of the saints between Christmas Day and new year (Thomas Becket), through new year, with its sense of leaving behind past griefs to look for fresh hopes, towards the first few days of January, when we'll be considering how we can bring the vision of Christmas into our daily life as everyday concerns re-emerge after the festivities. Finally, we reach the Epiphany, where we end by probing what treasures we can bring.

The poets whose voices accompany us on the road away from Bethlehem range from T.S. Eliot (yes, again, as he wrote *Murder in the Cathedral* about Becket), to Tennyson ('Ring out, wild bells…'), to W.H. Auden, who offers acute insights into just this moment in the year ('we have seen the actual Vision and failed / To do more…'). But there are others, from whom we have not heard before, such as the Welsh bard Nicander and the spiritual writer

Evelyn Underhill. They speak about what God has done, relating it to our growing sense of him, and how we can respond to his love. So Charles Kingsley encourages us to 'Do the work that's nearest / Though it's dull at whiles', assuring us that we might 'See in every hedgerow / Marks of angels' feet' (4 January). Epiphany encourages us to begin afresh, offering our 'treasures' – hopes, fears, griefs, commitments or whatever concerns us – this new year.

29 December (Thomas Becket)

1 John 2:3–9 (NRSV)

Losing our will
in the will of God

Now by this we may be sure that we know him, if we obey his commandments. Whoever says, 'I have come to know him', but does not obey his commandments, is a liar, and in such a person the truth does not exist; but whoever obeys his word, truly in this person the love of God has reached perfection. By this we may be sure that we are in him: whoever says, 'I abide in him', ought to walk just as he walked. Beloved, I am writing you no new commandment, but an old commandment that you have had from the beginning; the old commandment is the word that you have heard. Yet I am writing you a new commandment that is true in him and in you, because the darkness is passing away and the true light is already shining. Whoever says, 'I am in the light', while hating a brother or sister, is still in the darkness.

I can see why this passage from the first letter of John was chosen for today, the feast day of St Thomas Becket, which marks the day in 1170 when he was murdered by four knights in Canterbury Cathedral. It is about walking 'just as he walked': knowing God, obeying his commandments and abiding in him. But we know that much more is involved in this than just emotive uplift – like that of a management guru, with a message about practising what you preach or 'walking the talk'.

A motivational expert might write about the need for businesspeople to implement the values of a brand throughout its activity, in order for the product to have a clear identity that customers can buy into. So, for example, a DIY tool would need to look practical and be packaged to emphasise its usefulness, while a perfume would be sold on the creation of a more emotional mood, appealing to a different type of customer in the design of its bottle and the counter over which it is sold (I once met a designer who worked only on the appearance of the point-of-sale material), and the behaviour of the sales staff. Yet the writer of this letter goes much further: if we know God, we obey him to such a degree that we truly 'abide in him'. We 'live and move and have our being' in him (Acts 17:28).

Crucially, it is not just our willpower that has achieved this obedience, as it might be in the ambition of a business-person. It is God who has done his work in us: 'in this person the love of God has reached perfection' (v. 5). We have made the decision to allow God to come in (Advent prepared solid foundations for his coming), and now we abide in him, so that he can act within us. This can be enormously liberating. The fact that it is not by our own efforts that we dwell in God means both that it's not always a great struggle of hard work and that it's not an achievement about which we can boast. It is all down to God, who never fails. We need to keep on trusting him.

There is something of this realisation in the most famous version of the martyrdom of Thomas Becket, T.S. Eliot's verse play *Murder in the Cathedral* (1935). Much of the drama consists of Thomas being tempted to 'To do the right deed for the wrong reason', taking the shortcut to martyrdom by putting himself in danger. Instead, he needs to sort out his motivation and purify his inten-tions, realising that it is God who rules, not his inflated sense of self. As Becket says:

> ... *Death will come only when I am worthy,*
> *And if I am worthy, there is no danger.*
> *I have therefore only to make perfect my will.*

In the end, he learns to understand what martyrdom really is: 'The true martyr is he who has become the instrument of God, who has lost his will in the will of God, and who no longer desires anything for himself.' When we lose ourselves in God and allow him to work and love in us, we will really abide in him. It might take most of our life to reach this point, and we might realise that we are somewhere near it, all of a sudden, only when we have stopped striving for it. But we don't need to be afraid. As Becket says just before the knights kill him:

> You think me reckless, desperate and mad.
> You argue by results, as this world does...
> I give my life
> To the Law of God above the Law of Man.
> ... We have only to conquer
> Now, by suffering. This is the easier victory.
> Now is the triumph of the Cross...

By this stage, Becket abides in God to such an extent that he can move far beyond the values of this world and realise the point of giving his life. This is truly walking as Jesus walked.

For prayer

Lord God, who gave grace to your servant
Thomas Becket to put aside all earthly fear
and be faithful even to death: grant that we,
disregarding worldly esteem, may fight all
wrong, uphold your rule, and serve you to our
life's end; through Jesus Christ your Son our
Lord. Amen

Collect for Thomas Becket from *Exciting Holiness*
(Canterbury Press, 2003)

30 December

Colossians 3:12–17 (NRSV)

Clothe yourselves with love

As God's chosen ones, holy and beloved, clothe yourselves with compassion, kindness, humility, meekness, and patience. Bear with one another and, if anyone has a complaint against another, forgive each other; just as the Lord has forgiven you, so you also must forgive. Above all, clothe yourselves with love, which binds everything together in perfect harmony. And let the peace of Christ rule in your hearts, to which indeed you were called in the one body. And be thankful. Let the word of Christ dwell in you richly; teach and admonish one another in all wisdom; and with gratitude in your hearts sing psalms, hymns, and spiritual songs to God. And whatever you do, in word or deed, do everything in the name of the Lord Jesus, giving thanks to God the Father through him.

This rightly celebrated passage is wonderfully cheering, even though it gives us plenty to do. It's not the type of soothing message that suggests we just chill out and forget about our troubles; it has plenty of ideas for tackling them. But it doesn't feel like an aggressive, almost exhausting, uplift – mainly, I think, because, in a strand that follows on from yesterday's idea about our abiding in God, it is clear that God does the real work, not us. So we can invite the peace of Christ to rule in our hearts and the word of Christ to dwell in us richly.

Above all, we can invite all this to take place by clothing ourselves 'with love, which binds everything together in perfect harmony' (v. 14). The image of clothing ourselves with love is wonderful. It conjures up the idea of some-thing simple, which we can all do as easily as putting on our clothes in the morning, and also reassuring, as we enfold ourselves into a warm, soft blanket of affec-tion. But, as so often, it goes further, for it speaks to our purpose in life, which is to love.

Robert Southwell (1561–95) draws out something along these lines in his poem 'Content and Rich', which calls up themes of finding peace and joy in what we already have, rather than chasing after more and more new things. This seems particularly appropriate for the 21st century. Much is written now, by secular writers as well as religious ones, about the ugly side of consumerism, with econ-omies based on making us lust after possessions we don't need, so that, to counter this, a whole alternative line of thinking about happiness has been developed. This is the idea that we should rejoice in the existing things that we have and not compare ourselves with those who seem richer. Much of it draws on old ideas (including specifically Christian ones), and some of us might be tempted to say, 'We told you so,' as it all seems so obvious. But these are big forces that we are up against – so many vested interests and so much money having been invested in the systems that rely on our always desiring more than we already have.

Southwell's picture of an alternative is so appealing, though, that it might just help us persuade ourselves that seeking out the delights of what is already here could be worthwhile. He begins by emphasising that he has done nothing to deserve it. The idea of life as God's gift is fundamental: Grace, Virtue, Faith, Love and Hope are all freely given. Then he realises that he can find pleasure in simple things, that he is rich in what matters, and that he can grasp inner delights ('My heart is happy in itself').

I dwell in Grace's court,
   Enriched with Virtue's rights;
Faith guides my wit, Love leads my will,
   Hope all my mind delights…

My conscience is my crown,
   Contented thoughts my rest;
My heart is happy in itself;
   My bliss is in my breast…

This chimes with what even the most sceptical people have discovered when they try writing 'gratitude diaries'. The simple process of recalling, at the end of a day, a few positive happenings or feelings works wonders. Even those who instinctively find it embarrassing, or refuse to believe in any God to thank for such things, almost always end up being more positive. Many secularist psychologists, who wouldn't wish to be associated with Paul's words about being 'thankful' and 'giving thanks to God' (vv. 15, 17), nevertheless recommend gratitude diaries to their patients. They can see evidence that such activities work against many forms of depression.

Of course, serious clinical problems aren't that simple, but this is still a basic message that most of us need to hear, especially at this time of year, when we are pressed into acquiring yet more stuff, much of it under the cloak of bargain-hunting in the sales. Southwell points out the inherent dangers of having more than we need, when we become bound up by anxieties about losing it.

I feel no care of coin;
  Well-doing is my wealth;
My mind to me an empire is,
  While grace affordeth health…

He even goes on to analyse that very modern preoccupation of comparing ourselves with others, which cannot fail to make us unhappy. Either people will seem to have done 'better' than us (however we wish to define it), which makes us feel small, or we gloat over the misfortunes of others, which makes us terrible, unfeeling people.

> I envy not their hap
>   Whom favour doth advance;
> I take no pleasure in their pain
>   That have less happy chance.

So this wonderfully rich Bible passage fits this time of year, in which we look backwards and forwards. As we reflect on the past, perhaps with regret, we can confess our sins, forgive each other (v. 13) and resolve to keep finding, again and again, as often as we need to each day, our true purpose – to love. We can try thinking of clothing ourselves with love as we get dressed each morning. As a verse from the hymn 'Come down, O Love divine' has it, 'Let holy charity / Mine outward vesture be, / And lowliness become mine inner clothing' (Bianco da Siena, d. 1434). And we can have a go at doing everything in the name of the Lord Jesus, giving thanks.

For prayer

Glory to God on earth peace
Let this song never cease.

As I arise this morn
Christ in me be born

When I wash my face
Bless me with your grace

When I comb my hair
Keep me from despair

When I put on my clothes
Your presence Lord disclose

This is the day that you are born
Let every day be a Christmas morn

Glory to God on earth peace
Let this song never cease.

'*Incarnatus est*', David Adam, *From the Edge of Glory*
(SPCK, 2011)

31 December

John 1:1–10 (KJV)

Ring out the darkness

In the beginning was the Word, and the Word was with God, and the Word was God. The same was in the beginning with God. All things were made by him; and without him was not any thing made that was made. In him was life; and the life was the light of men. And the light shineth in darkness; and the darkness comprehended it not. There was a man sent from God, whose name was John. The same came for a witness, to bear witness of the Light, that all men through him might believe. He was not that Light, but was sent to bear witness of that Light. That was the true Light, which lighteth every man that cometh into the world. He was in the world, and the world was made by him, and the world knew him not.

This vital passage, which is usually read in churches on Christmas Day but is also set at other points in the season (such as today), can set the tone for reflections back on the gathering darkness of the Advent that has passed and, indeed, on the past year. It plunges us into an awesome sense of the immense universe, created by

God, and his light shining out of the gloom. This is the true light which can brighten each one of us. We walked in darkness throughout Advent, as the nights came in sooner and sooner, trying to turn away from our sins as we waited expectantly for the coming king.

Will you be glad to see the back of this year? Perhaps it wasn't as bad as a previous annus horribilis, or perhaps it still seemed like heavy going. But perhaps things are looking up, and there are small signs of possibility for the coming months. However I feel at this stage, I find it useful to review the highs and lows of the past twelve months and look to the future. Back in 2010, when I was asked to write about my hopes for the coming year, my first thought was to wish that my cancer wouldn't return, and it hasn't so far. So now I can set my hopes into a wider, less self-centred frame.

Some churches tonight will hold a Watch Night service. This is a way of looking back over the past, repenting and looking forward with hope. It is a particular feature of Methodist worship, but Anglicans, Baptists and others also hold it. It is a vibrant tradition in the USA, where it is associated with ideas of liberation from human slavery and freedom from the slavery of sin. Back in 1862, during the Civil War, slaves gathered on 31 December to await Abraham Lincoln's Emancipation Proclamation.

Even today, some black American churches encourage worshippers to see in the new year on their knees.

As part of their Watch Night service, some churches read out part of Tennyson's *In Memoriam*, passages from which we considered during the second week of Advent. Tennyson focused these particular lines on New Year's Eve, and they express tellingly for many people the sense of moving on from the struggles of the past ('The year is going, let him go') and welcoming the future. We can leave behind our losses ('the grief that saps the mind') and the troubles that have weighed us down ('the want, the care, the sin'). And we have the chance, which we should surely seize with both hands, to welcome a braver approach ('the valiant man and free / The larger heart, the kindlier hand').

> *Ring out, wild bells, to the wild sky,*
> *The flying cloud, the frosty light:*
> *The year is dying in the night;*
> *Ring out, wild bells, and let him die.*
>
> *Ring out the old, ring in the new,*
> *Ring, happy bells, across the snow:*
> *The year is going, let him go;*
> *Ring out the false, ring in the true.*

Ring out the grief that saps the mind,
*   For those that here we see no more;*
*   Ring out the feud of rich and poor,*
Ring in redress to all mankind…

Ring out the want, the care, the sin,
*   The faithless coldness of the times…*

Ring out old shapes of foul disease,
*   Ring out the narrowing lust of gold;*
*   Ring out the thousand wars of old,*
Ring in the thousand years of peace.

Ring in the valiant man and free,
*   The larger heart, the kindlier hand;*
*   Ring out the darkness of the land,*
Ring in the Christ that is to be.

Tennyson touches specifically on Advent themes in the last lines here, marking the end of the increasing darkness and looking forward to the coming of Christ.

For reflection

Can you find time today to reflect on the ups and downs of the past year and search for hopes for the new one?

1 January

John 1:11–17 (KJV)

Keeping that great covenant

He came unto his own, and his own received him not. But as many as received him, to them gave he power to become the sons of God, even to them that believe on his name: Which were born, not of blood, nor of the will of the flesh, nor of the will of man, but of God. And the Word was made flesh, and dwelt among us, (and we beheld his glory, the glory as of the only begotten of the Father,) full of grace and truth. John bare witness of him, and cried, saying, This was he of whom I spake, He that cometh after me is preferred before me: for he was before me. And of his fulness have all we received, and grace for grace. For the law was given by Moses, but grace and truth came by Jesus Christ.

Following on directly from yesterday's passage, these verses set the framework for our new year. If we receive the Saviour and believe on his name, God will give us the power to become his sons and daughters. Among all our hopes and fears for what is to come this year, nothing is

more important. We have spent all this time preparing
for Jesus' coming, and now he is among us, full of grace
and truth. We can rejoice in this. It is up to us to keep
welcoming him, each day, acknowledging his glory and
grace. If all this sounds rather abstract, we might think
about how a time of prayer in the morning – even if only
a short one – could set the tone for the day. Perhaps we
could pick one of the rich, short phrases from this passage, such as 'full of grace and truth' or 'of his fulness
have all we received', and ponder it for a few moments,
turning it over in our mind. It could seep into our outlook
on the day ahead. We can at least praise God and give
thanks for what we have been given, 'grace for grace'.

Today is also the Feast of the Naming and Circumcision
of Jesus, being exactly a week since Christmas Day and
so marking the obedience of Jesus' family to the Jewish
Law in having him circumcised on his eighth day, as a
sign of the covenant between God and his people (Gen-
esis 17:9–14). Traditionally it has been seen as the first
time our Lord shed his blood for us, looking ahead to his
ultimate sacrifice on Good Friday. Even here at the beginning of his life on earth, the end is already anticipated.

John Milton (1608–74) writes about this in 'Upon the
Circumcision' (1645). He tells the angels (the 'flaming

powers and winged warriors bright') to lament the fact that, already, the one who entered the world in glory 'now bleeds to give us ease'. How quickly our sins are crowding into his infancy.

Ye flaming powers, and winged warriors bright…
Burn in your sighs, and borrow
Seas wept from our deep sorrow,
He who with all heaven's heraldry whilere
   [some while ago]
Entered the world, now bleeds to give us ease;
Alas, how soon our sin
   Sore doth begin
      His infancy to seize!

Milton goes on to question whether this has happened because the law, under which our sins deserve punishment, is fair or because Christ's love is so excessive. His answer is both, with love having the upper hand: the law is just but God's love is even fuller, enough to overcome the demands of justice. We were rightfully doomed or judged to be without remedy, until Christ 'emptied his glory' and left his heavenly home 'for us frail dust'. He did this even though we continue to sin against God ('that great covenant which we still transgress'). So he suffered for us, taking upon himself the anger of 'vengeful justice'.

Finally, reaching forward already to his death, Christ puts the seal on his obedience for the first time in his young life, bearing an injury ('wounding smart') that will be dwarfed by his later sufferings.

> *O more exceeding love or law more just?*
> *Just law indeed, but more exceeding love!*
> *For we by rightful doom remedy-less*
> *Were lost in death, till he that dwelt above*
> *High thron'd in secret bliss, for us frail dust*
> *Emptied his glory, even to nakednes;*
> *And that great covenant which we still transgress*
> *Entirely satisfied,*
> *And the full wrath beside*
> *Of vengeful justice bore for our excess,*
> *And seals obedience first with wounding smart*
> *This day, but O ere long*
> *Huge pangs and strong*
>   *Will pierce more near his heart.*

However we view Christ's atoning sacrifice, most Christians can agree that he suffered to save us, the crucifixion being the culmination of all that he did throughout his incarnate life. This knowledge can keep us going through our own crosses and pains, which are mostly trivial by comparison. We can always look to the cross as our guide.

It is partly this that has inspired one of the most celebrated prayers for the new year, the Covenant Prayer used
at Methodist Covenant services on the first Sunday of the
year. It is often attributed to John Wesley, although he
reworked material from an earlier, 17th-century source.
It's hard to think of a better way to begin the new year
than to say this prayer. Try spending a few minutes weighing its words, phrase by phrase, thinking what it could
mean in your life over the coming months. How, for example, might 'Let me be employed for you, or laid aside for
you' be applied in my life?

For prayer

*I am no longer my own but yours. Put me to
what you will, rank me with whom you will;
put me to doing, put me to suffering; let me be
employed for you or laid aside for you, exalted
for you or brought low for you; let me be full, let
me be empty, let me have all things, let me have
nothing: I freely and wholeheartedly yield all
things to your pleasure and disposal. And now,
glorious and blessed God, Father, Son and Holy
Spirit, you are mine and I am yours. So be it. And
the covenant made on earth, let it be ratified in
heaven. Amen*

Methodist Covenant Prayer

2 January

Psalm 98:1–5, 8–10 (BCP/Coverdale)

'Everything became a You'

O sing unto the Lord a new song: for he hath done marvellous things. With his own right hand, and with his
holy arm: hath he gotten himself the victory. The Lord
declared his salvation: his righteousness hath he openly
shewed in the sight of the heathen. He hath remembered
his mercy and truth toward the house of Israel: and all
the ends of the world have seen the salvation of our God.
Shew yourselves joyful unto the Lord, all ye lands: sing,
rejoice, and give thanks… Let the sea make a noise, and
all that therein is: the round world, and they that dwell
therein. Let the floods clap their hands, and let the hills
be joyful together before the Lord: for he is come to judge
the earth. With righteousness shall he judge the world:
and the people with equity.

If yesterday was full of hopes, today is probably back to
reality, perhaps with a little bump. It's back to everyday
life, with work to do, whether paid employment, household drudgery or both. I don't think we should give up that
easily, as the choice of the psalm above suggests – 'Shew

yourselves joyful… and give thanks' – but I want to linger for a while with the return to normal existence after the holiday period. W.H. Auden sums it up so well at the end of *For the Time Being*, which we looked at during the third week of Advent. Writing about just this time of year, his Narrator describes the all-too-familiar experience of feeling that Christmas has somehow passed us by – perhaps a bit like Eliot's line from *The Dry Salvages*, 'We had the experience but missed the meaning', although Auden nails it specifically to Christmas:

> … Once again
> As in previous years we have seen the actual Vision
>   and failed
> To do more than entertain it as an agreeable
> Possibility, once again we have sent Him away,
> Begging though to remain His disobedient servant,
> The promising child who cannot keep His word for
>   long.
> The Christmas Feast is already a fading memory…

It can seem much easier to apply this feeling to others, especially to the once-a-year churchgoers whom we've just met at Christmas services. If only they would see the need to come more often; why can't they get the right idea? They can't be so frantically busy all the time… But such thoughts are lazy and unfair: we can't know what is going on in someone else's life. Auden's words have more bite closer to home: what have I done this Christmas to welcome Christ into my life more deeply? I seem to have skimmed over the surface yet again, glimpsing the appealing Vision ('an agreeable Possibility') and then turning away to my old patterns and preoccupations. I want to have my cake and eat it, remaining loosely in touch with God ('His disobedient servant, / The promising child…') without the drag of real commitment. I have failed to explore what it would mean for me to base my life on this Vision.

Anyone can be a Christian at Christmas, but this is the moment when it really matters, when, after the feast, as Auden goes on to say:

> … *The streets*
> *Are much narrower than we remembered; we had*
> *forgotten*
> *The office was as depressing as this. To those who*
> *have seen*
> *The Child, however dimly, however incredulously*
> *The Time Being is, in a sense, the most trying time*
> *of all.*

At such times, it seems as if we would do anything to avoid looking at ourselves honestly, despite what we have experienced at Christmas. Then, life fell into place in terms of our relating to God and the world around us: he wasn't just up there in heaven, and the world wasn't full of objects: 'Everything became a You and nothing was an It.'

> *Remembering the stable where for once in our lives*
> *Everything became a You and nothing was an It.*
> *And craving the sensation but ignoring the cause,*
> *We look round for something, no matter what,*
>   *to inhibit*
> *Our self-reflection…*

So what is the answer? Well, today's reading from Psalm 98 gives some clues: try praising God, thinking over what he has done for us. He has achieved victory over death and shown mercy to us. I've had a go at linking each verse (each one is a single sentence in the Prayer Book version) to an event in my own experience or one that I have heard about, thinking of a reason to join in the praise that is pictured here. So, for example, 'all the ends of the earth have seen the salvation of our God' prompts me to think about churches in different parts of the world where Christians show amazing faith, often in tough circumstances. Surely we can all think of 'marvellous things' (v. 1) that he has done for us or find a cause to be as joyful as the hills (v. 9).

Auden has some suggestions, too, about just how we can make Bethlehem part of our everyday life in our humdrum homes. He ends his long Oratorio like this:

He is the Way.
Follow Him through the Land of Unlikeness;
You will see rare beasts, and have unique adventures.

He is the Truth.
Seek Him in the Kingdom of Anxiety;
You will come to a great city that has expected your
    return for years.

He is the Life.
Love Him in the World of the Flesh;
And at your marriage all its occasions shall dance
    for joy.

For reflection

Can you think of three things you could change about your existence now, even if only in a small way, which would enable you to follow, seek and love the Way, the Truth and the Life?

3 January

Proverbs 4:1–9 (NRSV)

Seeking God's true Wisdom

Listen, children, to a father's instruction, and be attentive, that you may gain insight; for I give you good precepts: do not forsake my teaching. When I was a son with my father, tender, and my mother's favourite, he taught me, and said to me, 'Let your heart hold fast my words; keep my commandments, and live. Get wisdom; get insight: do not forget, nor turn away from the words of my mouth. Do not forsake her, and she will keep you; love her, and she will guard you. The beginning of wisdom is this: Get wisdom, and whatever else you get, get insight. Prize her highly, and she will exalt you; she will honour you if you embrace her. She will place on your head a fair garland; she will bestow on you a beautiful crown.'

Following on from the idea we met yesterday from W.H. Auden – about following, seeking and loving the Way, the Truth and the Life in our everyday existence – here we can see another of the ways we might carry this idea out. We might think that it's all very well to have high ideals but they do still leave us with a raft of questions about how exactly we keep to them in the ordinary round of life. So today's passage from Proverbs points to one of the paths towards this: the gaining of wisdom and insight.

It could sound old-fashioned and overbearing: obey what you're told, and be good – just at the time when, in the postmodern world, so many people have no time for duty and obedience to authority figures. But there is plenty of wisdom floating around; it's just that it has been repackaged for generations of citizens who instinctively recoil from being told what to do. So 'duty' is more likely to be rephrased as 'responsibility' to a specific idea or person, and deference to others has been reworked as some kind of earned tolerance towards them. There is also plenty of wisdom in the form of self-help books and hints and tips in magazines and on the internet.

Of course, we need to tease out what this wisdom from Proverbs might involve. One aspect is surely that of seeing more deeply. This is something we can apply to any situation. It means looking carefully; perhaps having the patience to wait; not being fobbed off with the superficial; getting a wider perspective, and bringing in the lessons of history, among other things. But all this is just common sense, surely. Is there anything that makes it godly? Much of our passage from Proverbs can sound just like any other philosophical instruction, such as the Greek thought that was current around the Mediterranean at the time of the apostle Paul – or even the instructions we give our children in places like school assemblies, where we tell them about being a decent chap and a responsible citizen. This is all airy talk of virtue and tolerance, without much sense of where these values are rooted.

God's wisdom is so much more than this. It is based on his being the creator of the universe, which he loves. Philosophical systems don't usually have room for God's grace and love for us all. Perhaps oddly, it is because God made us and the world, and loves us, that we don't have to strive so desperately to be good and nice to others. Of course we shouldn't be cruel, but we know that our efforts to be perfect will always fail. With God, though, we don't have to polish up our behaviour as if it's a test. It's not about who has the best manners: God is above all that. His world is much more grown up, although any child could grasp it. It is about responding to our Father's love.

Our love may be only a pale reflection of God's but it comes from his, so it has rock-solid foundations. We all bring that love into our whole outlook and all our actions; it colours everything we are and do, just as in God we live and move and have our being (Acts 17:28). This is what we need to ponder as we move through Christmas into everyday life.

Today also happens to be the commemoration day of a Christian who can offer some more suggestions about our response to the Father's love. Morris Williams was a Welsh priest, poet and translator who died on this day in 1874, in his 60s; he is known by his bardic name of Nicander. He took part in the revision of the Welsh version of the Book of Common Prayer, translated the Psalter into Welsh suitable for singing, and wrote hymns of his own, as well as many other works. But he is particularly remembered for bringing to his part of north Wales (around Bangor) the insights of the Oxford Movement. He used his poetic gifts to encourage revival, and his hymns had a profound impact on the spiritual lives of many people in Wales. So he was someone who worked hard with the talents God had given him and applied them wherever he could see they were needed, in ways that reached out to those around him.

This sounds like true wisdom and can suggest a pattern for us – to use what gifts we have, even if only humble ones, to be part of God's work. So, even if we can only make tea, run a stall, welcome people or stick down envelopes, we all have our part to play.

The lines below are from one of Nicander's hymns, translated from Welsh by Naomi Starkey. He writes of some of today's themes of relying on God's grace and looking to the Spirit to nourish us ('With the lifegiving rain of your Holy Spirit / You refresh the Church'). Drawing on God's gifts, we can all flourish in the Lord's vineyard.

For reflection

You planted your holy church, Lord,
in a world that is so unclean;
A tender vineyard, green, and fresh,
in the midst of a desolate land.

It bursts with abundance, not of this world
but the planting of the Spirit of Jesus;
Not earthly dew, not its false fertility,
that scorches the growing green.

Not only the dew of the heavenly realm
Brings increase to its strength;
Not only the rain of God-sent gift
Ripens to the full its fruits.

With the life-giving rain of your Holy Spirit
You refresh the Church, your vineyard,
Until its blooms are many and fair,
And its fruits like the garden of paradise.

Hymn 138, *Emynau'r Llan* (*Hymns of the Church*, 1997)

4 January

John 1:35–42 (NRSV)

'Do the work that's nearest'

The next day John again was standing with two of his disciples, and as he watched Jesus walk by, he exclaimed, 'Look, here is the Lamb of God!' The two disciples heard him say this, and they followed Jesus. When Jesus turned and saw them following, he said to them, 'What are you looking for?' They said to him, 'Rabbi' (which translated means Teacher), 'where are you staying?' He said to them, 'Come and see.' They came and saw where he was staying, and they remained with him that day. It was about four o'clock in the afternoon. One of the two who heard John speak and followed him was Andrew, Simon Peter's brother. He first found his brother Simon and said to him, 'We have found the Messiah' (which is translated Anointed). He brought Simon to Jesus, who looked at him and said, 'You are Simon son of John. You are to be called Cephas' (which is translated Peter).

We continue with the theme of carrying the faith of Christmas on into our everyday life, with the calling of the disciples. Here, later in the same first chapter of John's gospel as the passages we read on 31 December and 1 January, is John the Baptist identifying Jesus as the Lamb of God, telling his own disciples about him. One of these followers of John is Andrew, and he then brings along his brother, Simon Peter. This process has often been held up as a model for how evangelism can work, with its searching questions ('What are you looking for?' v. 38), the invitation to meet Jesus personally ('Come and see', v. 39), and the idea of introducing him to our closest friends and family (Andrew 'brought Simon to Jesus', v. 42). All these stages can be important parts of the process as people come to know Jesus.

But what chimes with our themes at this moment in the Christian year is the notion of Jesus breaking into everyday life. If we are thinking about how to live out our faith seven days a week, and how to take the experience of Christmas into the new year, we will need to explore this idea further – and it has to go deeper than those magazine articles that appear in the late summer about taking our holiday mood over into September. (The answer, by the way, seems usually to be something along the lines of giving yourself treats, like exotic meals out, and displaying your holiday souvenirs where they can spark memories.)

For us as Christians, if we are saying that God has truly arrived at Christmas and is the centre of our being, then our daily life – on a Friday or a Tuesday that may be chilly and dank – has to be different. It needs to start and end with God and be focused on him. If we look again at the three stages that the disciples went through, we might see, first, that Advent was a time of working out what we were searching for, when we were looking forward to God's coming. Then, with 'Come and see', we need to spend time recalling ourselves to the presence of God ('they remained with him that day', v. 39), before finally we can bring others to him.

The middle stage – being with God – is where we are now: it encompasses our prayer, worship, Bible study and spiritual reading, which we can do any and every day. It will lead on to our reaching out to others and, whether explicitly or implicitly by the quality of our actions, introducing them to our faith. Any acts of generosity or service – even merely keeping the business of faith out in the world as a phenomenon – obviously need to be done for themselves, wholeheartedly, without looking over our shoulders to see the impression they are giving. I hope it doesn't seem too embarrassing to see such actions, no matter how humdrum, as offerings of love for God.

The classic, best-loved poem about such offerings is George Herbert's 'The Elixir', which many of us know as a hymn:

Teach me, my God and King,
In all things thee to see...

A servant with this clause
Makes drudgery divine;
Who sweeps a room, as for thy laws,
Makes that and the action fine.

There are others with this theme, though, including 'The trivial round, the common task / Would furnish all we ought to ask...' by John Keble (1792–1866), in the hymn that begins 'New every morning is the love'.

Charles Kingsley (1819–75) adds another dimension to such themes, linking our everyday work, be it ever so dull, to God's care for his world. This is from 'The Invitation' (written 1856, published 1889):

Do the work that's nearest,
Though it's dull at whiles,
Helping, when you meet them,
Lame dogs over stiles;
See in every hedgerow
Marks of angels' feet,
Epics in each pebble
Underneath our feet.

For reflection

What seemingly dull piece of work could you see in a different light today?

5 January

Ephesians 3:8–12, 14–19 (NRSV)

The love of Christ that surpasses knowledge

Although I am the very least of all the saints, this grace was given to me to bring to the Gentiles the news of the boundless riches of Christ, and to make everyone see what is the plan of the mystery hidden for ages in God who created all things; so that through the church the wisdom of God in its rich variety might now be made known to the rulers and authorities in the heavenly places. This was in accordance with the eternal purpose that he has carried out in Christ Jesus our Lord, in whom we have access to God in boldness and confidence through faith in him... For this reason I bow my knees before the Father, from whom every family in heaven and on earth takes its name. I pray that, according to the riches of his glory, he may grant that you may be strengthened in your inner being with power through his Spirit, and that Christ may dwell in your hearts through faith, as you are being rooted and grounded in love.

I pray that you may have the power to comprehend, with all the saints, what is the breadth and length and height and depth, and to know the love of Christ that surpasses knowledge, so that you may be filled with all the fullness of God.

This passage, the first part of which the church sets for today, takes us further in the ideas we have been tracing about our everyday life in Christ. It focuses on the grace of God, which we need to draw on within ourselves. This is our inward strength, an undeserved gift from God to each one of us and the wellspring from which all else flows. No matter how weary or hopeless or untalented we might feel, the truth of God's love for every single one of us really can fill our hearts. Whenever I find the going tough, uninspiring, dull or just not seeming to be worth the candle, I think today's passage is a good place to turn.

This is Paul's prayer for the Gentile Christians, and applies just as much to us now. Paul speaks of our 'access to God in boldness and confidence through faith' (v. 12); he asks God that we may be strengthened, that Christ may dwell in us and that we may know his love. God's strength and love will sustain us through the boring bits of life, this January and beyond, as well as the extremes of high and low.

A poem, 'Immanence', by the spiritual writer Evelyn Underhill (1875–1941), takes parts of this notion of Christ dwelling within us and puts them together with the idea (met several times during Advent and Christmas) of Christ choosing to set aside his heavenly home (his 'starry wings' in Underhill's poem), out of love for us, in order to come alongside us in our little existence. Each of its three verses begins, 'I come in the little things', and the last one runs like this:

I come in the little things,
Saith the Lord:
My starry wings I do forsake,
Love's highway of humility to take:
Meekly I fit my stature to your need.
In beggar's part
About your gates I shall not cease to plead –
As man, to speak with man –
Till by such art
I shall achieve my Immemorial Plan,
Pass the low lintel of the human heart.

Jesus, as we saw on Christmas Eve, 'in whom all our hungers are satisfied', fits his 'stature to your need'. As is movingly and touchingly portrayed here, he becomes humble and meek, like a beggar pleading with us, in order to reach out to us. This is why we can know him 'in the

little things', even as they all get going again (and perhaps
threaten to drown us in their inconsequentiality) here in
the new year.

A more familiar piece of verse, the Tate and Brady version
of Psalm 34, brings out these qualities, too:

Through all the changing scenes of life,
  In trouble and in joy,
The praises of my God shall still
  My heart and tongue employ.

Oh, magnify the Lord with me,
  With me exalt his name;
When in distress to him I called,
  He to my rescue came.

The hosts of God encamp around
  The dwellings of the just;
Deliverance he affords to all
  Who on his succour trust.

Oh, make but trial of his love,
  Experience will decide
How blest they are, and only they,
  Who in his truth confide.

Fear him, ye saints, and you will then
*   Have nothing else to fear;*
Make you his service your delight,
*   Your wants shall be his care.*

So here is a pattern for us to find God in the range of our little experience (in trouble and joy), to praise and thank him for his past mercies and place our trust in him for the future, throughout this coming year. Our 'wants shall be his care': God will look after our needs if we let him, and if we trust him enough to offer them up to him.

For prayer

Father God, thank you for loving me throughout the little things of my life. Help me to sense the breadth and length and height and depth of your care for me and for your world. Amen

213

6 January

Matthew 2:1–3, 8, 10–12 (KJV, abridged)

The treasures we can give

Behold, there came wise men from the east to Jerusalem, Saying, Where is he that is born King of the Jews? for we have seen his star in the east, and are come to worship him. When Herod the king had heard these things, he was troubled, and all Jerusalem with him... And he sent them to Bethlehem, and said, Go and search diligently for the young child; and when ye have found him, bring me word again, that I may come and worship him also... When they saw the star, they rejoiced with exceeding great joy. And when they were come into the house, they saw the young child with Mary his mother, and fell down, and worshipped him: and when they had opened their treasures, they presented unto him gifts; gold, and frankincense, and myrrh. And being warned of God in a dream that they should not return to Herod, they departed into their own country another way.

We have finally reached the crown of this part of the Christmas season: the coming of the wise men at the Epiphany (literally, the 'showing') of Christ to the world.

We have already looked at part of the most famous poem about this event: T.S. Eliot's *Journey of the Magi* (see the reading for 4 December). The ideas we considered then tie in with what we have been reading over the past few days – about how to go back to our previous life after the experience of Christ at Christmas. We have the choice of being submerged yet again into our old, tired, limited existence or of drawing on the vision to forge a new, more hopeful and less fearful life:

> *We returned to our places, these Kingdoms,*
> *But no longer at ease here, in the old dispensation…*

The story of the wise men also gathers together other themes of the Christmas season: like the shepherds, the wise men come, worship and offer gifts; like Jesus and the holy innocents, they face Herod's murderous wrath. The first element here can form a pattern for us now. During the past five weeks, we have been moving towards Jesus, at the same time as he has been coming to us. We have pondered the paradoxes and mysteries of his incarnation – thinking over the mind-boggling ideas of his leaving his home in heaven to become a tiny, vulnerable baby. Poets have offered insights into all this, which can only foster awe and worship from us. So, like the wise men, we have travelled (if only in our minds) and worshipped. Now we can also offer our own treasures.

On Christmas Day, we read how the shepherds brought 'each of us his lamb' (Richard Crashaw) – suggesting, perhaps, how we can offer our everyday concerns and the things we cherish, such as our work, our household cares and our relationships with those immediately around us. Now, it is more a case of offering the special things. In another poem about the wise men, 'The Gift', the American poet William Carlos Williams (1883–1963) writes of:

> *The rich gifts*
> > *so unsuitable for a child*
> > > *though devoutly proffered,*
> *stood for all that love can bring.*

A few lines later, though, he seems to be saying that the gifts, standing 'for all that love can bring', are part of a wider response to God:

> *The ass brayed*
> > *the cattle lowed.*
> > > *It was their nature.*

> *All men by their nature give praise.*
> > *It is all*
> > > *they can do.*

So the poem ends:

> ... *The wise men*
> *came with gift*
>
> *and bowed down*
> *to worship*
> *this perfection.*

This suggests to me how we might see our treasures – given by God to us, and now to be shared with our fellow creatures – in the wider context of worship. We offer our whole selves, including all our talents as well as our short-comings, to God who loves us.

So these gifts are our gold, frankincense and myrrh: they might include our money (even if we haven't got much, we are richer than many people in the world); our worship and time spent in prayer and spiritual reading (frankin-cense being used in worship as a sign of the prayer of the saints, Revelation 8:4); and our dearest hopes, fears and griefs (myrrh being an embalming spice and a symbol of death).

Epiphany is a good time to ask ourselves about our spend-ing and giving; our commitment to God, church and our fellow Christians; and also what we are really looking for, what we are afraid of and what sadnesses drag us down. There is so much to think about here, so perhaps we should just pick one of these 'treasures' – hopes, fears, griefs, Christian commitment, money or whatever fits our particular concerns this new year. I could ask myself, where am I at the moment (not comparing myself with others so much as taking an honest look at my circumstances)? Am I really content with my situation? What exactly is holding me back from offering my treasures to Christ? Can I think of one or two simple steps that could bring me closer to doing this? So, for example, perhaps I am weighed down by fears for the future, for myself and my family: can I set those anxieties in the perspective of God's love for me? I could try praying about them specifically, and possibly discussing them with a Christian friend, pastor or spiritual director.

For reflection

Now is only a beginning.

Questions for reflection and discussion

These questions can be used by groups or by individuals on their own. Some groups might not have as many as five weekly meetings at this time of year, so I have designed each session as a stand-alone event.

Obviously the group meetings will work best if everyone has read all the daily material, but this isn't absolutely necessary, as I have picked out just one of the readings from the week and one of the poems that goes with it. The questions are based on this reading, while also drawing more generally on the themes for the week.

Another approach would be for a group to gather together and discuss which of the readings the members found most interesting or challenging.

Week 1: Surveying the territory

Psalm 23 | *Ash Wednesday* by T.S. Eliot (readings for 5 December)

- What fresh aspects does this version of Psalm 23 suggest to you that other versions don't?

- What do you value about Psalm 23 (in any version)? Does it have particular associations for you?

- Have you ever thought seriously about facing death? If not, could you use this psalm to address and allay some of your fears? Try picking out parts of verses (such as 'all my midnight hours defend' or 'through devious lonely wilds I stray') and thinking about what they could mean to you now.

- I have quoted from *Ash Wednesday* by T.S. Eliot: 'Teach us to care and not to care / Teach us to sit still.' What things do you need to stop caring about, so that you are able to sit still?

Week 2: The untwisted path

Isaiah 40:26–31 | 'The Revival' by Henry Vaughan (readings for 12 December)

- Do you sometimes feel weary in your Christian life? If so, why? What are the things that make the feeling worse – and better?

- Are there specific difficulties that stop you from trusting in God's promise to renew your strength (Isaiah 40:31)?

- Try to think of times when changes for the better have suddenly come about – in individual lives, in the life of your church and in society generally. Did these changes come out of nowhere or were preparations made beforehand and seeds planted?

- Which particular aspects of such revivals can you most thank God for?

Week 3:   Tracking God's Wisdom

2 Kings 2:9–12 | *'Morte d'Arthur'* by Alfred, Lord Tennyson (readings for 15 December)

- At this time of the church's new year, and in preparation for the new calendar year, which aspects of the past year would you like to carry on into the future? Which aspects would you leave behind?

- When you think of people who have influenced you in the past, can you thank God for the particular things that they taught you? Also, can you reflect on the ways in which you needed to apply these lessons on your own, away from those who helped you?

- What does the image of the earth's being under God's rule ('the whole round earth is every way / Bound by gold chains about the feet of God') say to you about your life today? How do you see yourself fitting in to this picture, in relation to God?

Week 4: 'That holy thing'

Luke 2:7–14 | 'A Hymn of the Nativity' by Richard Crashaw (readings for Christmas Day)

- Can you think of any ways to make this gospel passage seem fresh in your mind, despite the fact that you may have heard it so often?

- Are you able to break off from Christmas festivities – if only for a few minutes – and spend some time praising God for his gift of Jesus Christ? If you find this hard, could you try reading 'A Hymn of the Nativity' by Richard Crashaw, either on your own or in a group, taking each line slowly and pondering the words?

- 'Each of us his lamb will bring' says the poem. What can you offer: from yourself, with a group of others and as a church?

Week 5: Back to the new life

Psalm 98:1–5, 8–10 | *For the Time Being* by W.H. Auden (readings for 2 January)

- Can you think of one 'marvellous thing' that God has done for you over the past year – as an individual, in your family or immediate circle and as a local church?

- What can you do to 'show yourself joyful' this new year?

- Are you concerned that you might have missed the meaning of Christmas? Does it seem like a distant memory that has already been swallowed up in the busyness of life?

- If so, can you think of one or two ways in which you could bring the experience and meaning of Christmas into your everyday life, this new year?

Further reading

There are many collections of spiritual poetry, which offer wonderful treasures if you're willing to dip in. Two substantial anthologies are:

Donald Davie (ed.), *The New Oxford Book of Christian Verse* (Oxford University Press, reissued 2003)

Peter Levi (ed.) *The Penguin Book of English Christian Verse* (Penguin, 1988)

In addition, the following arranges poems alongside Bible passages:

Robert Atwan and Laurance Wieder (eds), *Chapters into Verse* (Oxford University Press, 1992)

And these two volumes have poems chosen according to their relation to the church's year:

Mark Pryce (ed.), *Literary Companion to the Lectionary* (SPCK, 2001)

Mark Pryce (ed.), *Literary Companion to Festivals* (SPCK, 2003).

Other wonderful anthologies include:

David Winter (ed.), *The Poet's Christ: An anthology of poetry about Jesus* (Lion, 1998)

R.S. Thomas (ed.), *The Penguin Book of Religious Verse* (Penguin, 1963)

G. Lacey May (comp.), *English Religious Verse: An anthology* (Dent/Everyman, 1937)

Ruth Etchells (comp.), *Praying with the English Poets* (Triangle/SPCK, 1990)

More specialist volumes, which I've used in writing this book, include:

Sweet's *Anglo-Saxon Reader in Prose and Verse* (Oxford University Press, 1967)

Douglas Gray (ed.), *A Selection of Religious Lyrics* (Oxford University Press, 1975)

M.S. Luria and R.L. Hoffman (eds), *Middle English Lyrics* (Norton Critical Editions, 1974)

R.T. Davies (ed.), *Medieval English Lyrics* (Faber, 1963)

F.E. Hutchinson (ed.), *The Works of George Herbert* (Oxford University Press, 1941)

John Carey (ed.), *Milton: Complete shorter poems* (Longman, 1981)

Christopher Ricks (ed.), *The Poems of Tennyson* (Longman, 1969)

T.S. Eliot, *Complete Poems and Plays* (Faber, 1962)

W.H. Auden, *Collected Longer Poems* (Faber, 1968)

There are also, of course, many modern Christian books that draw on poetry. Some people have found the following books useful and have recommended them to me:

Robert Atwell, *Celebrating the Seasons: Daily spiritual readings for the Christian year* (Canterbury Press, 1999) and *Celebrating the Saints: Daily readings for the calendar of the C of E* (Canterbury Press, 2004). These are readings from sermons and spiritual writings, including some poetry.

L. William Countryman, *The Poetic Imagination: An Anglican spiritual tradition* (DLT, 1999) examines Anglican spirituality through poets such as Herbert, Donne, T.S. Eliot and R.S. Thomas.

Esther de Waal, *Seeking God: The way of St Benedict* (1999, Canterbury Press). She ends each chapter with poems, prayers and quotations.

Richard Griffiths, *Poetry and Prayer* (Mowbray/Continuum, 2005). This is a Lent book which discusses poetry in general and also examines particular religious poems.

Malcolm Guite, *Faith, Hope and Poetry: Theology and the poetic imagination* (Ashgate, 2010). He writes about a range of poets, including Donne, Herbert and Hardy.

David Impastato (ed.), *Upholding Mystery: An anthology of contemporary Christian poetry* (Oxford University Press, 1997)

Alwyn Marriage (ed.), *New Christian Poetry* (HarperCollins, 1990). Another anthology.

Michael Mayne, *This Sunrise of Wonder* (DLT, 2008) and *Learning to Dance* (DLT, 2001). I have enjoyed these two especially among his books, which draw out great riches from poetry and other writings.

Mark Oakley, *The Collage of God* (DLT, 2001). The author quotes poetry throughout the book as an approach to exploring faith. Mark Oakley has also edited *John Donne: Selected Writings* (SPCK, 2004).

Index of poets

Index of poems

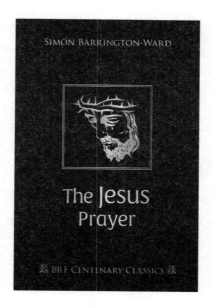

'Lord Jesus Christ, Son of God, have mercy on me.' This ancient prayer has been known and loved by generations of Christians for hundreds of years. It is a way of entering into the river of prayer which flows from the heart of God: the prayer of God himself, as Jesus continually prays for his people and for the world he loves.

The Jesus Prayer
BRF Centenary Classics
Simon Barrington-Ward
978 1 80039 087 4 £14.99 HB

brfonline.org.uk

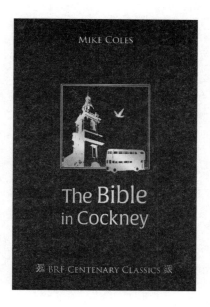

Read how Jesus feeds 5,000 geezers with just five loaves of Uncle Fred and two Lillian Gish. Or how Noah built a bloomin' massive nanny. Then there's always the story of David and that massive geezer Goliath, or the time when Simon's finger and thumb-in-law was Tom and Dick in Uncle Ned and Jesus healed her. *The Bible in Cockney* is a very down-to-earth 'translation' that brings scripture out of the pulpit and back on to the streets.

The Bible in Cockney
BRF Centenary Classics
Mike Coles
978 1 80039 090 4 £14.99 HB

brfonline.org.uk

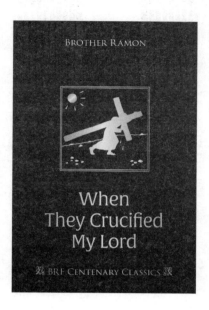

On this journey from Ash Wednesday to Easter Day, you are invited to become a pilgrim with Brother Ramon. Each day there is the opportunity to stop and reflect on the gospel story, drawing insight from the experiences of those who were there during the events of the first Easter, finding inspiration and strength for the greater journey of our lives. Suffering and glory are intermingled in real human experience in this book, which is designed for personal and group use, for Christians of all traditions.

When They Crucified My Lord
BRF Centenary Classics
Brother Ramon SFF
978 1 80039 088 1 £14.99 HB

brfonline.org.uk

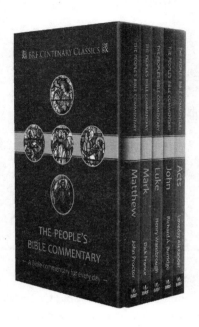

The People's Bible Commentary series presents scholarly insights in straightforward terms, aiming to instruct the head but also to warm the heart, and pointing to how the truths received can be applied personally. This special boxed set edition brings together five best-loved titles in the series to mark BRF's centenary.

The People's Bible Commentary:
Matthew, Mark, Luke, John, Acts
BRF Centenary Classics
978 1 80039 093 5 £39.99

brfonline.org.uk

Enabling all ages to grow in faith

Anna Chaplaincy
Living Faith
Messy Church
Parenting for Faith

100 years of BRF

2022 is BRF's 100th anniversary! Look out for details of our special new centenary resources, a beautiful centenary rose and an online thanksgiving service that we hope you'll attend. This centenary year we're focusing on sharing the story of BRF, the story of the Bible – and we hope you'll share your stories of faith with us too.

Find out more at **brf.org.uk/centenary**.

To find out more about our work, visit

brf.org.uk

Sharing
the **Story**
since 1922